The Course

The Course

Ted Greenwald & Charles Bernstein

ROOF BOOKS
New York, NY

ISBN: 978-1-931824-84-2
Library of Congress Control Number: 2020931233

Author photo by Star Black, October 7, 2008

Chax Press published a selection of the poems as *Short Course* (thanks to Charles Alexander); and 24 Hour Chapbook published a selection as *In the Course* (thanks to Joshua Medsker). Other poems were published *The American Journal of Poetry, Big Other, Black Box Manifold, Fell Swoop, Plume, Read On,* and *Thresholds.*

This project is supported, in part, by an award from the National Endowment for the Arts.

This book is made possible, in part, by the New York State Council on the Arts with the support of Governor Andrew Cuomo and the New York State Legislature.

Roof Books
are published by
Segue Foundation
300 Bowery
New York, NY 10012
seguefoundation.com

Roof Books
are distributed by
Small Press Distribution
1341 Seventh Street
Berkeley, CA. 94710-1403
800-869-7553 or spdbooks.org

for Tom & Val

Contents

Perfect Air

Put book down
As if
Spine up
You think

Look out, window
See what
Shave hours
Where's that

What's was
Where the fuck
You say
Is Carmen

Phone rings
That's then
There the fuck's
Say Hello

Carmen
Dead air
Wait a sec
Hang up

When can
Lean to
And fro
Bear weight

Lend some
Up late
Then gone
Passing double

Bubbling troubles
Wall, eye never
Lent loan, come
Hammered, then home

Read thru see thru
You do who
Makes a third
What's second, on

Curve
(Love the fastball)
Today toast tomorrow scones
(Yesterday's yesterdays)

Mustard summer sand
But said nothing
(Nothing says nothing
As good as hitting

A blank wall at light speed)
As Fi
Saying as
Fi as a

And so ask
(Repeat fire)
Then forgot to
(Repeat fire)

Edge on set
Like I used to say
Surf tree's wave
Not the same

Like the feel
(Breath covets)
Snow cover your
(BUT)

Narrow path phone tap
Lose the applicable
Some treat outline
Quicker than a

Silk exhalation gala
Only now it's
You
(Remembering the time)

Don't
(Notational elides)
Know
(Spell it out)

What
You
Don't
(Spilt verdict)

Know
(Say AH!)
Twine ball
Twin yarn

And the fuselage
Repairs mystifications
Shout out to
Sullen strangers

Even
More
So
Now

Sounds midday meadow
Tuckered watch globs
Youth is speaking
A void is listless

Surreptitious squawk
Eyeballs
Lurk along, alone
Musty

Taken up rather
Inches get to feet
Thin underline
Breeze wigs leaves

(Come) unclue
(Unglued)
Rustling somersaults
Somnambulists delight

Right around
Rotary, votive
Crescendos don
Incendiary

What would
(Think)
Pony That Walks
Too latte

As in tango with me
And you'll throw
The dice
Overboard

Schools cruel
Tools enviable
You apparent
Mimic, empathic

Game skin
Chastened
Street quite
Darns universal

Out of
Otters
(Slide, quench)
Is it

Or isn't it
The moment right
One day
Wake up

Won't
The gun went off
As guns will
When left

To their own
Device
Color it
Triangulated

Says Carmen
Who appears
Like the return
Of the depressed

In a twinkle
Visit world of
A new movement in hair
Tiptoe each breath

Angling for disadvantage
Via storyboard
Incongruence
Besots debtors

Round about it
As available
No answer
On this line.

Editate

Read the land
When you can
Own mercy
At disposal

Dawn into valley
Shed in shadow
Thus raising the car
Fear undone

Hail, bent chief
Slim divide
Current motion
Lickety spilt

What's life
Not this
Says Carmen
To cork

Giant ice coffee
And
Why
Not

Plastic sheet scaffold
When
Know
They

Stand on ether
Or neither
Abutting what
Have you

Or have not
(In the clear)
Solid air
Unbuttons

Loosely attached
Cat
On/off
The fritz

Not
So
Long
For

Heard it
Reported said
Little more color
Though who says

You drive
Get out
Flights over
Day begins

Just when

Read the Land

Incongruence
In a twinkle
No answer

To question
Not forgot
A round

Like the return
When left
Out of

Night for tonight
A smidge
Seeing eye

Wake up
Overboard
Right around

Smack
Bon Ami
Said the guy

Eyeballs
Even
Shout out to

Flooring
On Loan
Or Aims

Don't
Only know it's
Like the feel

Then forget to
Curve
Bear weight

Hang up
That's then
As if

Exactly my taste
Breathing space, yup
On lingering loan

Get back promise
Lost in Palisades
1956

Or aims
Aimlessly
You tell me

Better selves
At least not yet
Highways of CA

Isolated tomato
Visitors from
Another world

Word refill
Fills agree, fingery
On loan

Dime for a dollar
Flushed with
Inconsequent adulation

Flooring
Calculations for net
Nothing

They say
BUT
Said

Said the guy
In plain air
Just

Tell
Irene
Bon ami

And a bowl
Of ice
Work

Shifts
Make it
OW

WO
Fack
Thack

Smack
Between
Time and

Tell
Comes up
A smidge

Seeing eye
Night for tonight
Swing and miss

Ladder to nowhere
Dream
To stick

A round
Keep
In in

Touch
Midweek
Hamstrung

A basic
Unit of
Humidity

Foregone
Humility
Never forgiven

Not forgot
To question
The answer

Buzz
Beat
Pirouette.

Pirouette

Reasonable daubs
So
Shot
Him

Think
Of
To
Do

That
Was
To
Done

How
About
Some
Ice

Cream
Please
Address
Me!

See I've
Just
About
Got

Vistas
For
Horizons
Unsung

Sort of
Tanking
Tantra
Totality's

Tardy
Ground
Out
To

Third
In
The
First

Down
Looking
Mess
Around

In
The
Dirt
Shaky

Free
Blue
Sky
Ancestors

Brain storm cellars
Going on about
Sibilant
Misunderstandings

(Indelible)
Whosoever
Endeavor
(Spunk)

Goes
The
Diesel
On my

Bad
Mouse
The (the)
Cat

Once
You're dead
Too late
The hora

(The) the
Fact
That
(Verdict music)

Dogear earmarks
Open
The
Door

Faces
Angelic
In
Their

Disgust —
You know
My
Life's

A
Spoken
Book
Written

In
(A)
Language
Fit

For
Thieves
Just
Taking

What's
Theirs
Hours
Bounces

Sunny
(?)
Day
As

Whose
Fortune
Mends
Plays

Loot
Like
Love
Needs

Eyes
Level
Changes
Turn

(The the)
Sleight, slight
Chin
Scum

Music
Mars
Elective
Care

(Chair)
Announces
Radiant
Flesh

Fit
Flit
Sit
Quilt

You
Be
Right
Down

I
(The the)
Elevator
Goads

Immaculate

Early
Warning

Wolf
(Says)

Mollusk

Success
Defines
Upholstery

(Fest)

What's
An

E

Pock
Peoplely

Let's
Faces
Less
Graces

Remove
To
Music
Just

Like
As
(As)
(Always)

Like
And
So
Are

You

Mums
The
(Word)

Cantorial
Tones

Flagrant
(if) (as)
Flipper

Goes
To
Tonic

Who has
Graced
Disgrace

Molting
In a

Keyhole something
A good start
Nice little cloud run

Go To

Looks like clouds
Those clouds
Something serene

No feel
For changeup
Call time

(Images crowd body)

Space to take
Windows for doldrumslatin

Or the day-glow sheen
Of recollections
Comes dropping

Like confetti
From rockets

(Compare to what?)
Signed note moments

Quote

Over-the-top better
The perv circles back

In infinite compensation

Lost is the telling
Layering locutions
As if style

Was going out business

Grizzled
Monuments
Momentarily

Enjambed in
Viscous
Rockettes

Think of to say
Say
That's funny?

A maybe cloud
Mental sandpaper
Smooth edge

A younger wha
Officials create

A perimeter
A new movement
Inspects

Long-range
Anthro scene
Discrete

In hair

Turn to stone
(A blue)
Afternoon sentence

(Or)

Clause
Which
Lilts

(Polly perorates)

Phantom reruns
Now indecipherable

(Body parts / Memory sways)

As seat of
Pants
Kicks in

Doing what
Spose a mores
Lean din

Do into others
Stocking trade
Big steaks

Tide out
Less (less)
Put away stuff

Leave looking
To the lookers

Others impose
Guarantee of uncertainty
Never sure of

Refer to incendiaries

Sunday
As a weekday
Not rest

Brakes for upset
Non-closure deal
Return to the mildew

Often

Buenos dial
More
Thin than

Want

Hop over
Into Queens
Customize

Floatation
Relies on
Riptide

As well as
(Well)

Sketch could've
Stretch talk about

Moment in between
(Raises) (hackles)
Intent on
Migrant passage

No sense
To speak
Of (of)

Blurts commission

Over
Out of

Solid irresolution
Calm upset
Gold ash

Field to mouth tidbit
Jack's BINGO
Apple excite

Core

Stays as such
Trusts no one

Slip on
Soggy air
Neat thread

Over and above
Sifts

What be
Doing

Between
Subsequent & prior

Music from TV
Drifts up
From traffic
Down said street

Pungent toss
Imitates
Lonesome medley

Brain
Hair
Pitter
(Don't tell me that)

Pat a butter
Color to face

Where work
(Blue)

White haze

Forfeit make poifect
Peccadillo in square
Sensation of

Lateral movement

Arrival of
Marmalade
Twice tip

Say what?

Toe dip
Shimmy shammy
Shame on youse

Squint
Then became
An again, child

Swings echo

Young leaves
Cover the trees
Cover the trees
Cover the trees

Cloverish rock
Pronoun on it, no
(Open door)

Richard is a song
Eternal youth
Stings

Humming whiplash
In two timing

Sings

Forfeiture of purpose
On a dime
Swept

Myriad
Haystacks
Abide

Branching into festering
Hope
Poolside

(Ingredients make the porridge)

Alongside the canal

Wind gust
In time
Wheelers misspoke

Property
Twinges
(Return
Mandates)

Throw strikes
Which tree

Goes with peach
(Heart précis)
Libelous guarantor

The pest whisperer
Take the wheel

Symptoms

A buffet
Against a crush
Avenge

Where suction
Boomerangs
'Round

Varmint heroes

Can't go
Into details

(Her silver sweater)

Dishwash algorithm

So
Maybe
That's it
It stands

To reason
It don't

Sit right

Garnishing inapproapriation

Teaser for
What remains
No hooks

Sliver'll
Belt
Intaglio

Where's Steve
Now that
There's a break

Customary custody
Not this time
Then whose

Not in the name of
If I ever say
Moment then not

Heading
(Higher into hills)
Confusion of source

Catch fur
(Catch fur)
Collocation of reminders

Though never forgot

Trip to
Wolf ticket country
This is

Isn't good
Breathing

Room

Nagging
Joyance
Aside

Get out a here
And
And

(Stiffness)
Open a spine

(Dale)

Change (lane)
Call or click
Mate
Cleaves

Relief
At last
Sounds

Sharp silver flats
Weighed down
Like something

Been said what
Been here
(Been) spoked

Fat chance
(Beef for)
Sloped motion

Charm under (irk)
Fluent (lull) amasses

Succor Punch

Like confetti
As if style
Turns to stone

As seat of
Dear lead
Stiffs

Pithier
Whit haze
Stings echoes

Abide
Haystacks
Myriad

Swept
On a dime
(Or)

Lifts
Which
Clause

Avenge
Symptoms
Where suction

A tale of Whoa
Nellie square one
(Message) a

Known loser
All cute
In court

Spit into face
All about
A U

Another nice day
2nd movement
How bout snack

Tangy thrids
Is peligrosso
Means huh?

A what-about-me
Somebody
In a Dodge

Medical street
Work out for
The Beast

I'm about to stare
(Revenue of the wasted)

(Base relief)

As in
Bad day at

(Welcome to)

Huh?

Flat rock
Good sipping surrogate
Equate other options

For loan officer
On the dole

Dips as in

Freedom's phantom

Mistress to the whorl
Like show tunes, like Billy

(William to you)

I am in a sea drift
Of my own quaking
Chiseling wind
(The larceny of the trees)

A fog horn sounds the silence
More

(More)

Test in turn
Initial blowout
Say so

Bad news
Rain to the left
Right, nice

Slice of sluice
(Sorted by initial entry)
Forked living

Smoke out
(Can you dig?)
Right word for
(A little louder this time)
Yesterdays

In stacks
The Muse of Blame
No-see-em

Broken solace
Sample meal

"No notion, no lotion"

On demand snow
Clue
Lesson musical

Pertinent to straw
Low rider

Large AT
Chairs
Word each extract

(Wanted doing)

Impaired derangement
Along lines of

A word
Just some letters
In the mail

SWAKKK

Say them like
Unhinge
U230feelfree

Among
Weathers
Go on
Among

Hence spoken

Pass the passing
Time woozy
Clue cloudless

Not
If not when

Take dawn
Move away

Nother crash
Nother mind

Betters locate
(Absolute traction)
In middle of

Brackish sibilant's
Incunabula engine

Rotates bearings
End run among

Nosedives
Fluoroscopes
Mid-life nap

Treacle
In the thread's
Nosegay

(I did not)

Simonize the deflection
In case
Arthur asks

A holiday of notions
Wrapped up in crinoline

Eat out disorder
End game
Famishes

A sandwich moderne
Light and eerie

Quells quail
In hiccup outfit
Salubrious emanation

Nose fit

As in

semaphore
Obliges
Disrobing

Face it
Original donor
Get

(Séance)

Outta here
Around

Phlegm blue
That's to spell it

Aboard
Outbound flight

Donor noted

Smacks of elastic retrofit
Smudges tinting

U turn you

Nice day
So what!
Fuck off

Foggy hard drive

A flare state
Flamingo loll ball

(As Hilda keeps watch)

Drawing
Brushes with
Whatever

That whatever

Forget this

On stage
A moveable feets

Frets
Stress
Pullover contraption

Sings a race
Wanting to trace

Including

High cloud
(They say)
Breeze, fly

Uneven keel
Bright screen
Semi-precarious

Going by the book
(Chapter and worse)
Let's git

Troubadour

Obligation
(Strike zone)

It's funny
In this d d dream
N n nothing specif

Icky

Abler than a bedbug
Lose way
Head inside

Lose way HEY

(Melody loading)
Dream scraps
Rain tours

The great something
Else
On brink of
The eyes, okay?

Fiddle fiddles
Take my vittles
Take me to Fair

I once knew a girl
Named Tangerine, Tangerine
Now I have no hair

Some hill
Formerly Sam
Drop degrees

Slam to the ground
Deeper than before

Go dark
Geezooie
What the . . .

Shoulder Shoals

Chronic beauty burns muscle car
Outside era's motor
Thousands coasters island nation
Incriminates incendiary valor
Sweep up
With spools of loops
End sentence Mahatma Kane
Rues reality all to quickly
Use WOW frequenting
Mannish squeamishness
Spire out of country
Much as it expends
A person coloring book
With hooks and crooks
Beauty's rule wrinkles
Down the drain
Do you do after done
And then no more
As we know it
Or knew it
In time for wake.
Windchill needs fixed
Autodrift activated
Land's door ways
Off and on
Chips at C
Minimizing
Day same next another
On a tumbling spire
Fit day's book jacket
Runs aground
Door number 3
Subsumes
Bother whatnot
Those who's to say
Clouds dark on bright
As in

Suede

Journeys never end
The way you thought
In the middle

Who wore what
Building blotter backdrop
Coughdrop

Anthrobscene fodderdall
Absorbs comeuppance
Quicker than a blink

Late dog lite
Phew tear into
Necks stop

Craning around
Jewell-encrusted
Porcelain mannequin

Where waaa
At
Add green

Stashes silt
Apart
Audit spare

Wet towel air
Roof peak volume
Head clear heading

Anywhere but here
Nowheresville at warp speed
Now you've found it

The next level
A person of interest
Cap no-fly price

At any rate
Movement
Cold, stare, hard

Talk about awful
Tweak idle lawns
Wit game in skin

As the eyes had it
And then it was the mind
But now

Even alone
That's it
Baby baby

Solo trap 'ere loosen lay
Trip hollow 'pon pale fume
Settle none in twisting gown

For health reasons
Top 10
Is this why no

And ails no more
Nor sings in spring
Real sure

Fingers cross
Nice weather
Treacherous, that said

What is never thunk
Sometimes
Or not at all

Beguiles stand on star refuse
Today's dream wordly dish
How's about XtraXtra lunch

Or deny, deny, deny
All that can never be true
And already is

Double dutch rain
Preposition helicopter
Noun noun

Sworn sane
As in a puddle
All is muddle

Eloquent cloud vagues
Moisturizer (non adjective)
Verb drape

Not that you'd care to notice
Percolating on purpose
Back to the bar and then some

In real life
The true story
Lines lingering

Across borderless aisles
Ensnaring the guile
Gods made so we

Four seam heater
Motto cheers
Redemption damper

Go this way and not
Glimpsing in glimmers
Luckless, limber

Cast voices
From snake brain
To nipples

Abrogating arrangement's annulment
Like annealed tires
At the Indy 500

Morning diorama
WW2 over and over
Fucken thing whole

By halves
And then some
And then some

Lots of OF phrase
Back teeth pearls
Shape wet inks

Not now maybe
But in a little while
If the breeze holds

Music grat ciels
Leather winter's awl
Hole in snow's belt

Catapults entropic bestiaries
Lisps with delicate motes
Elevates uneven boundary

Get up make bed
Get up make bed
Get up make bed

Just me and my radio
Awake all night
Moscow in range

Suede II

Pre perfect
Live girls Live police
Bring an eh

Slowly, as if falling
And the ground falling too
As if slowly

Heavy day
Many grays
As if hungry

Air as heavy as water
Grays even darker, richer
World awaits

Couple kissssing
Their mouth tastes
I'm there

I'm not
A million miles away
Just to be here

Movie family
Souvenir spoons
Evening

As the steps get steeper
Thoughts lighten
Melt the air

Sunset redundant air dreams
Click in sun at poolside
Lounge wandering mind

Ever over whatever
Sways and swarms
In charms of lurid calms

Incongruous, sensate, cozened
Smacked down to fiber
Sullen romance

Have a pulse
Hip locket up
Pix right at you

Then the pull
Then the pall
Then the after

Something
With a potato
Day perfecto

Slides
In its imbroglio
On wings of sand

Glad
Have, had
Time width

Slumping in my chair
Sewing flips
Indigo repair

Stop speed shop
Driving a matzoh
What's this

Inching alongside
As in caboose of the train
Elsewhere

Smell heat
Crack window
Slip stream

I only seem to be dreaming
The others know better
Just passing down the line

Nowadays italics
Look up   Not on
Scratch

Fast feint
Doubleback at the quarter
Insulation exultation

A lightweight mask
Continuous hydrangeas
Stories doesn't go away

Simply impossible
Retails obligation
To semiconscious enclosure

Comes next
Turn in at
Someish shrubish

Warts on call
Framing
Radiating patter

A flower nominal
Side effects, what's
Go way back, up, Doc!

Slack decoding slack
The better by the mile
No return

A smile
On the foot
Let's go, Dad

And we're off
Just like
That was

Sen Sen Cha Cha

Water sound
Jumps in
Mid sandals

Rippling under the hood
As a slipcase rewards
Looking elsewise

Relax throat
Around sound
A word means

Just about nothing
As if on a stroll
So many as ifs

Hold tongue
Stranger's hand
Word for

In a manner of
So who was
Insufficient unto

You ever
Siddown
Say anything

In the edge world
Curving behind
Goddamn big gulch

Didn't say
Left elbow bend
Goes around

Fellow feeling
Say what? I've got
All the tin in the world

Could-it clouds
Easterly blues
Last seen

In dirigible
(How do you spell that?)
Come on, come clean

Door as portal
Postal a (gum and) go
A-game (with me) outrigger

Longing for longing
But banking on next stop
'll be the next one

Wait up
Nice out
Step up

Focus behind
Feel what's were
What's when

Useless use-to
Name comes up
Way when

Leaning on left
Hurts enumerating
Wisp of wish

Flesh out
Curves in space
Sounds how

’bout that, she, it
Flying without trespass
On my so-called lawn

A new word a day
A new day
Word for word

Inebriate of sound
Debauching dawn
In search of night

Monsoon ringtone
Deliver weave levels
Heal thigh’s danger range

Athwart a lack
Beside the hey
Amidst such rubble

Unrunging bell
Beyond cloud U
Funny cater feel

Absent any honor
Fear gnawing at heart
Then back again

Swingline same line
Bread and without pause
Butter up emboss

As in: it’s all a toss
Count me out
’til the melody

Going on behind
Getting off and on
Note for note train

Remains insoluble
At the door of
Instinctual abhorrence

Is how treats
Unsigned be have
Kweep offering

Stuff, stuff, stuff
Stuff, stuff, stuff
Stuff, stuff, stuff

Come to Think of It

Spits
Out
Real
Fall
High
Clouds
In
Which
Says
Spikey
Flutter
Curve
Away
This
Time
Early
Morning
Flight
Echoes
Echoing
Echo
Plot
About
About
Time
Insufficiency
Grating
Paper
Plate
Drone
In
My
Slowmation
Out
In
On
Then

Of
Among
E
Follow
Cap
Along
Away
Aways
Don't
Mention
It
Stuck
In
Place
Rude
Mopeist
Motes
Low
On
Floats
Didn't
Oh!
Paint
You
Bet
(Yet)
Slip
Sure
Said
When
Got
This
Whatever
Appear
Knot
Armed
Or
Naught
Hover

Street
Sails
Spin
Splash
Speed
Knaw
How
No
Guessing
Passing
Mention
Consult
Cat
Stretch
Out
If
This
Blotter
Sky
Removal
Takes
Two
To
Screen
(The)
Article
Just
As
When
Face
Lit
Aperture
That
Them
There
Tow
Close
Case
Floating

By
As
The
Big
Picture
Only
Your
Just
Dog
Gone
Own
It
Sure
But
Hands
Kurds'
Way
Slakes
Sure
Thunder
Hidden
Willing
Fight
Then
Dodge
Which
Lift
The
Lid
On
Crocked
Bologna
Be
Up
On
Ever
Not
That
Blink

Voice
Tire
Ever
In
Cloud
Do
Say
Whomever
Pleased
Was
Slip
Clip
Sleeve
Swept
Forge
Gone
Dough
See
Dough
And
Away
You
Easy
How
Pretty
Go
Stay
Simply
Sip
Sofa
Roof
Back
Of
Mind
Or
For
Whom
Where
Snipers

Pay
In
What
Way
Say
Lots
Gains
Come-on
Heels
Mope
Steal
As
As
Don't
Worry
Only
If
Or
Even
See
Arc
Rave
Down
Dim
Aisles
Careful
Service
Dimples
Gump
Up
Shimmies
Arrival
Window
Moon
Only
To
Recoil
Rainy
Patter

Heart
And
Then
And
A
Breezy
Mix
Under
Wandering
Sky
Wake
70s
Bleak
Murk
Chirps
Longing
Hi!
In
60s
Sludge
Makes
Music
Tonight's
Some
Remembered
Chance
Less
Balance
Big
Eyes
Warmer
Glassy
Almost
Still
Of
That
Time
Drifts
In

Edge
Curl
Off
Brick
Anywhere
But
Up
Days
In
Weeks
Flap
Like
Geese
Ear
Toot
Roof
Smoothly
Sawing
Prime
The
Swell
Mome
Where
Swept
I
Own
Boat
Unknown
Til
Time
Can't
Sh(o)w
(The)
R(oo)m

Leaving the World

More fun
Drift cloudy
Air edge
Slaps Comedy
Between Laps
Grain's grain
Trick into
Blinking lites
Whoa, Nellie
She say
Who went
Got there
Doing so
Looking thru
So you
Guess that
Me too
Say so
Has been
Made more
On way
Has been
Made more
On way
Then that
Or That
Can say
This if
It but
Their of
Nowhere anyway
Floor bites
Out of
Back away
Disposable aside
Do it
Sloughing (some)

Magic oats
Braid grit
Why was
Was what
Wheels whom
(Say what?)
(Time's up)
(Get going)
Sound not
Need speak
Even usual
Sway, so
Seeps, still
To deeps
Door closure
Well, sure
Fall unfold
Like likeness
Unblend now
Knows no
Drawing board
Parallel English
Do then
'round troubled
Bends into
More notion
Papers push
Número carefully
Laughter ravioli
Pain fusilli
Wades wish
Worries warrant
Sardines R
The nuts
Pix accident
When inclemency
Borders on
(Radio off)
City pat

Upper 1/2
Stagger trigger
Incontrovertible currency
Renders mute
Other occasions
Scale tips
Toss talk
Fur firsts
Imbibe regret
Flat's forecast
Amassing plain
Back early
Spoken smile
Sip look
Vagrant laughter
Echoing amidst
(Stolen chance)
Figure (twinge)
Flip phoney
Coffee office
Adverse plan
Contends with
(Kept mum)
Train gumdrop
Voice level
Grab baggage
Accuracy ablated
Fits foment
Surety gliders
Legs, fall
Come across
Wandering dreams
In bins
Left for
Want, willing
Call waiting
Notary rotary
Open notebook
Ascends dusty

Walkway gathers
Flight only
Remark stairs
Hawser titles
Ropa dopa
Sunk in
Incommensurable blink
Eye stains
Way back
Invisible gaze
Tie bow
Gets me
Every once
In a
Rappel down
Je m'
Applied waiting
Past accounting
In Jimmy
Waits elation
Say it
That's it
Did it
Nah, but
Gee, hm
Whiz, with
And then
Again (all
Together): limits

Laugh, Clown, Laugh

When was it
Or was it
Ever, moisture
Metabolizing

Pause to C
Necessary selldorm
Repeat family
And counting

Arguably nobody
Then the sting
Try not to . . .
Who say what

A hand
A voice softener
A soffit
Grommet winks

Plies on plies
Recalling
Jaded jades juggling
(As flounce)

On way back
                    Pen wink
                                        Only hope
            The door

Closes
Once
Then
Gone

Call over
                A chair
                A man asks
        Footsteps shower

Impertinenancillary
                             (gived
  (before
              outage
                Busy baby
     Every second one
                                    Considering
It's the tooth

Will's the way
                             (Steps
Monopolize
              Mortgage's valiant snooze

Grow more oars
             The short story
  Lace ex fingerettes
          Min

Fixtures of a
Sullen elation
              Archives
Mists

     Done in
Spoken fees
                        Wobbly Gang Green
              Beauty committee

And then
And then
And then
And then

Tell so
Here's a question
Credit for hooooo
Rest a score did

A ring around a
Zoom
(Omelets for two)
(Try me

Ask, smiling
Foot contact
A fuss office
Come back, shirt

) or some time tells
over the out
fruity but stop short of
nuts

All be clear
Work on
But you know mic
Memory tenders

Rippling happen
Mill aside the stem
In send up
Remembering when

Walking lonely road
Landing plane
Folk cuss groupers
Saw sea spritz

Angling
Suppositions in lock-
Step
Overtion

A suite
Don't asterisk
Guy name Dad
Knees isn't

Even when tries
Bet that goats
Get a banana!
A boy and a man where . . .

                        Walking in
         Shoes
                    Danger going four words
Behind curvature

As in notation of
                       (fallen
I've got my
I'll get my

That's
           My my my
                 Hesitancy
      Fall daisy chai

As in: up to you
More than likely
And when ready
(Fold here)

                       Came back to back
Don't even know preposition
    Gimme for a give me break
        For children crossing

Lots of bah hah bah hah
             Brands
Exotica for local
Hay (hey) Hey!

Back seat
        A head
Argumentative
                Exactly doing

Meme of some kindness
                                (as a)
                Slept intergemically
Coulda maybe, maybe could

Cut for go we
Trouble much
Watching kepi
Hat tennis

Hand over intransience
Milk and morose
                (Testing)
(One Eight Seven)

Was thinking
                Much to hope urn
   Empathy be seated
                                        Grass roots ain'ts

Exactly if the case
Were what it was
Note what it ain't
(So say so)

Week oof
                  And you?
     Dredge an estuary dirge
           Fuck this shit

Grudgingly content
               (Must be it)
Smoke or ire?
               (Who'll take the hit)

Creature For

Wooden stares
                              Takes all pillows
     Movies

                         Just to be talking
                    Numbers on this tits

or tilts
moment of

gotta getta gotta
increments
                              (inclements)

                              so
say
              (s0)

Demo butt
     Studio crow
          Sure works

                         Come out no luck
  Gonna use gonna coulda

lurch
leer
loom
lip
loquation
'uminosity

              Summer)blip
In comb,
              Lulu!

Speedy hair ledger
Knock on bank
Thrown off baloney

Picture dollA
Me make more mentality

(fiddle, fiddle, foil & quibble)
exit: mercenaries, apothegms
she's still swell
o! where goes
in bits & bows

Long awful look-see
Makes talkee too oo long
Love to

Left house
Field skits

Flummummiating
(Pick up the phone, Martha!)
includes
don't forget to

this bill of lading
Bundled and waiting

Napkin mouth
Get look at similitude
Remnant rain very heavy
Heavy
Slip off

As in modern art isn't modern
I told you too many times &
sundry laundering
Manicure desire

(

fools follow fools
but so do I

Journey step
Delicious fud
Front dwawing
Home fleer
Nice ring message

Tuning unguent forensics
Floor's the bottom lime
In nefarious pose
Winging it, willy nilly

Floods

Good knuckles
Friend at snap
Desk facing East Wind

Hurt your filings

Take holdover
(flip
(argue
(arrange
Clips

No matter what happened
Even if you said no
I never knew that

Take a straight answer
Turn leftover
View, check out
Counter clutcher

Sitting on an easy chair
Tap out

What
We now know
Take home box
Immediately

ZONE INTERDICTION
, says the aunt

(Maybe they were right about fluoridation and the commies invaded our water supply. That would explain a lot.)

Put pants on
Narrow opinions

Minutes
See?
OK
Offa Deano
As(wan)(a)lot damp
en

She the
Yeah, like
A little
Hair closer
Comeuppance

Waada, wadda and not a drop to

Still flummoxed by the radio
Heart in hand (or on
Belies stutter of flies suturing
butter as the army advances/retreats/advances

Looks that way
Click off
Hands phone face
Surveilling

Way better, better
Truck starts at truth stop
Quarantine, money back
Paperback mass Marquis Garage
Ganges home
I Swear
(ate a

Going on sheer sheer
Advanced flippance
Augers annul endemics
in the garden's lace

We gonna do
Got a plan
Be nice
Or
Be a gone

Pick up
Can't miscellaneous

(plain in the . . .)

Focuses Autumnal bloomers
As in backside backways
(Behave, they said, or else live
half clawed, heart calling)

Over the hill is a veil
And on the other side

Moods
Whispers

Any trouble
Ride out

Fit music
Drive around

Insatiable cowering
So good you can no longer take it

Is that right?
                    Good taste
            Squeaky nodding
                              Broken Lynn system
     False toothsome
                         Sound Bit-O-Honey

Hollering into a noiseless wind
            Make-do, make-up, marking
   (. . .)
Tools are made for fixing things
But not for you, not for me
Skies belie the ground above
Tug of day's swept fights
                          & grim rewards

'Til we take it up again

Angels on the Run

Fat change
))hits
Mordant histories
a scant glance
echoes
florid obsequies
never more than

Incorrect dosages
Intercept by researcher
Up in fronts voice
Thumbs fold
Er, awl power pont
Cross eyed nunchuks
Nothing to using

Re: Fw: _Fwd:_Re:_Re:_Hello_from_
Re: Fw: _Fwd:_Re:_Re:_Hello_from_
Re: Fw: _Fwd:_Re:_Re:_Hello_from_

Insensible of you to say so
Indispensable of you to lay low
(the eyes had what?

Slip by slip, slope by slope

Sideways
Stop   What good
Willow as aluminum do
Won't shut the fuck
Like how
Porch lite
Recluse smoke

As they go, so she goes, so he goes
Punching up
          (7, 23, 81 . . .)
Anytime you call
          Where in the skylight skylarks
Toss & fret in
          Six
  foot bins
          ))Randy! Last warning!
aglows with impertinent
          resistance.

Leverage

Smoke gets in your tires
I swear
Small body
Pow
Ripe brow
Little by latter
Grinding up mistakes
Into the sweetest powder
Originating
See a 360
It's many stones
Peep don't know
How much a dollar costs
To invent or buy
On closeted markets
Of bread and lye
Eat up
Go on
Coulda woo
She still sails by
(That's who)
And what's up or out
On face look
Radio find out
Pretty sure
Then again
Not same
Tilted aggregator
Loom large as
Happens works
Lawyer good got
Ratty catchy
Engulfed by fervid barometer
Sultrifed carols booming
In stratified superfluities
Enuf eyebrow
Metal tiptoes

Oh, what's that
Gonna star
Whoooshhh^**$!!Bllllaaaatttt&&^%%@!
Tssaaassssghgty!!&^>!Galllllluuppp*^!@+=>
Perspicuity its own demise
Swiss cheese
Play Better Chance Records
Do you do spindle
Attaboy
Crusts into first
Trolling for air bubbles
Or bust, flux
Millinery-Indubitable complex
A single grooves
Wait, roll of bills thumbnail
Go way back
Weft in throat (say)
Or frogs in boat (say)
Twister twisting toward me
Torn lock
Say what!
For sure call
As what
Name As
Gimmie bag so sweet
Janes my name on it
Flows the caustic
Round the curves
Hanging back
Half moon cutie call
Clue fingerling
Smite duffer clues
A tendency taken
Taken away
A zillion squillion
(Of bread and lye)
Earned loss don't fade away
(For sure call)
A squillion zillion

(Blast and fuse, fuss and trust)
About to happen
By missed steaks
Meat glance
Brush toe
Come back white
Sky do not disturb
Hoe home feel curbs
Like air the sound of
Promo
It's many moans
(Chorus of blanks)
On face lack
(Chorus of thanks)
Grinding up takes
(Chorus of banks)
In stratified fluidities
(Chorus of tanks)
Do you do spangle
Buzz, floop, freeze
Came up
Nip picked
Shoulda incense
Night streets
Yeah, let's wait
Catchy wandering
Nap sake
Water dawn
Really Lily
Sheened instance
As "shoulda" Lily
Or "catchy" keepsoothe
Amounts to 356 x quid
(Liberace)
Moonbeam gone bonkers
Playing the black keys
(Yeah, let's)
Special occasion
She quit

Drumming fingers
Smoking porch light
Tuff questions
(Yeah let's)
Sheened insistence
Amounts to real Lily
Napped beam (wolverine?)
Dim in pocket
(Should've)
Pickets mercury
On duty as of
A waitress
Wooden surfaces
Never ending little more
Fees and penalties
That little restaurant
Slipping napkin petals
Local (read newspaper)
Talkative bouquet
Pouring back forth
Made in scratch
Mental pancake
Slightly hot
Was on
Shelves
(Disheveled rope-a-dope)
Burning with a flexed
Contagion (wink!)
Any time better than
Bludgeon (slink!)
Don't even know if
(Helen can you hear this?)
Trust and ferry
Granted overtime recusal
Wasting in beset
Quit it
Hands free seasons
On veer
A shrug

Frown foregone
Is that right?
Coulda step outside
A nice guy
Missed missive
Fleshing out clouds
Nasal more'n anything
Design garage
Look alike beaches
Twinned with monotony
Aggrieved sumpturaries
Toodling on a pipcdream
Fit for the brimmed
Masses (fat to tile)
(Soak up the . . .)
Deflationary fairy ring
Rims about the lard
Spew 'em with soft focus
Listening
Nodding
Spare time work
Up from there
Born back them
Time off: drink
Ratted out
The light come on
Knew to work
Drink from knowledge sconce
Waddn't good at anything
Unnerstan science
Look in good
Nice rug
It's a twin twin
Cocktail chaise long
Softee
Thrink from knowledge stone
Knowd work
Tint off: slurp
In from there

Massive intellectual trailure
Often in space (spacey, spacing)
Surreptitiously obviate (obvious)
((Oblivious)(
Non-con-sequential
)(Storebut))
Easing into it
In bright white abandon
A good one
The new name
A mirror play
The last thing
Three chords
Facing it by turning
Around and [   ]
(Just tell it like you
Thought you think it)
Armed by precarious
Joie de vivre
And 5-dollar cologne
(Kool Aid)
(cool it)
Smack against
Tire iron
Said, The President
Working together
How the world
Possible lotion
Skin feel good
Wipe out flakes
Don't wait call 8
No podium
Unless I lend you the one
I'm standing under
Undulating like as remains
A fragment of the farm
I told you last time
(You know)
When no one was listening

Even while
Eaves litter the trees
When talk 2m
Do well with
On book tour
This is 2nd story
Half of brain
Elect The Pez
Big horn tweep
Yawp yawp
Better messenger
With houses
Time drop out
They're at 0
Spell out
Cutting up
Crowd going
Part of the reason
A better 1/2
(You know)
Fried even when the bacon
Laid an egg (doggone)
Sputtering poses
Deft as Moses in
Hot pursuit
Discombobulating aroma
(Spatula times eight
Dusts the surfeit)
On these weft street
Stray grazes, rumored
Reproach
Feet away
Lights nasty
Up look to time
Two time
Gonna partition
But who who R m
Make nice palms
Humidity

Voters get to see
Change polls
Deadpan pretty sure
Oh my gosh
It's a runaway
Sue who
Me? My radio?
Acclimatator?
Dead span fairly certain
Humility
Sport of reason
Moments fly into radiator
Steam, wish, whim
You name it
Salud or sallow
Cups on cups
(Intransigent transience)
Stand up
Fill eyes with tears
Wrote the book
Columns
After 9/11
Readers now than
Diff res
Goodness heart
Capital hill
Was at game
Put price tag on
Lying recall
Beholder eye
Gives back
Almost nothing
In the mix
Plate glass widow
Repletes
Roast remnants of
Last life
Listlessly
On the fend

See up, say over
Who's this guy
Nothing personal
Outside groups
So far cycle
Is or not bowling
So so needle
So on average
Bang same date
Rule out
Two foot own
Edge rate negative zero
Smack athwart
"Ye follicles invade
My tumors," cries
Mary, Bill, hell spent
On turqoisosity
Sublates rumor
"It's no secret," she
Keeps saying
Forsooth
Lots of quirkiness
Frame story house
Trouble widder troot
Stop me
Before I kill again
A personal tree
Breaking numbers
Morning sun's
Personal advisers'
Snazzy underwears
Wha?
Real lime
's the most unreal
Or sometimes it
Seems to suggest
A turn is the most
Straight away thing
You can hop onto

Or is it hip, split
Splish, in spiraling
Disclosure of lurkish
Adumbration, facing
Inward toward
(Forsooth)
Even as we soothe
(I'd like to give you)
To breathe
Simpering, sled
Easier in shell
(Turn to the)
Ear crawls outta
(Lime's lit)
On a TV
Or baulkwalk
Yon sabre metric
Chandelier
(Before I will again)
Drip drip drip
Into the murky
Loathed diplomacy
(Repletes)
Frequency kiddie
Forensic episodes
Allow six weeks
(N.B.)
For delivery
(Candelabra)
Within the us
Or their, them

Double Tap

Main Street disarray
All chem afterlife
Something's gaining

Endemic patalife
Churning boost
In love of mocha

Terrible trues
Drapes back
Keep remove

As mores wane
Fashion tains
Garbled cycles

Face glass
Walk in
Find out

A murmur
Wall off
Below brow

Tha
Raisin
Tell you

Or not
Or even-steven
Or resoluteness

Fills
Inambulate foostiary
Brazen betrayal

(Betrothal
Announces quipped
Jellificaton

Pent-up for a thousand
Moments, fecund flip
Fogs forever rips

Not leaving
Without who
Referee

Big bite
No foul
Previous

See doctor
Side effects
Today's weather

This is last week
Looks like early
Previous

Dunes
Imbue
Sleepliness

Solvent for the moment
Rolling in lacklusterousness
(tone!)

Guardian stares
deep into
(   )

Brace self, closet
Othernesses, fealty
Bounds behind

Pop up again
Reddish
(Unwritten)

Learning
            Curve
      See on flim

Laminated clouds
Reply gosh woods
Peak cola

Bam
Cash back
          Belly up

Gripppling the (a)
                    Baggage
Shut / Shut / Shout

Grimly at game
          Slim slice of
  (Just a, justa)

Sincerely rim
Torques filament
(Soupy?)

Command out of excavate
          (Bench press retort)
[Mags?]

Starts with intercept
                          On outside
  Puts on brakes

Go back
Last week
Stylo

Rule down
One more look
@ 13

Nerver batter
Gazooks!, she screamed
Into her innter logic

While
On the outside
Couldn't find it

Sheer
Beamishness in the lurch
Thursday on

Simpers tempers
Sweet tenders allay
Gridiron echelon

Take up sex
Plato Interior
Wait cloudy day

Upper hinge
No roof skim
Metallic green

White interior
With Ari
Kaching CA

Late 60s
Alternate universe
Foops flops

Floops incompadre
Elemental sojourn
Cuts three ways

Saturate
Obliterate
Declination

Ennobles quagmire
(Corner salooned)
Frequently mummery

Stalls past reticent
Heliopathy
((>?]])

Look into crime
Define CLOUDS
Poll numbers rise

So happy
Only election
Nice smile

Look good
Young
Man sweats

The wiredest thing
Logicless
More than ever

All day listen
One more season
Woodpecker laff

Litttterbuff cropes
Amoong ammonunition
Flaying way lakers

Jets (are it?))
Fit for mulling
((quilt?

Ambers its rump
So close to immoculatte
Sourcer (sorcerror, so sure)

Gobs, that's it,
Streak
Mind rays

Cloud cover right back
Showers wind back
Nice sunny

Allegation
Caption
Recharge

No interest for month
Poppy slop
Health of others

Workers exposed
Syllable delivery V hic
Sleeve slo momo muumuu

Ammo Domini
Fix it or
It fix you

Yolk the fox
(says the . . .)
Relentlessless

Mummy, on flute
Sphinx bass
Sure say something

About the flight of man
(Five classic brews)
Sure make hey

Sure thing
Go back
Yours do

But weight
The song
She is heavy

You're kidding, no
                    Go for it again
     Same it

                     Car sophically
Winterize quasi freebs
    Below wish canto lopes

Quasi-julip devioration
        Mints excerpts
 Erupt minor bathos

Tributary tribulations
                                (triangulations)
        Forswear

Galapagos magic, mimicking
            Ichabod hootencies
Sheer crust

                      Embraces occipital
Farmer's cheese
       In slow houses

Chord
            Chord
                        Chord

Scream, yo
                       Same gun
                       Come home

Let’s see
Some. More drums
The walk walk

(Solo)
On balance
Installment purchase

As wisp becomes
    Clear swear
Abounding

Agent of &@”:/(
Cleaves to tidal
Rift)incorrigible

        Derringer
Silo rigs rope
  Slap prance

Souciant warning
        Times out
Nature’s bluff

As big as life
        In this town
  For awhile

                What’s this
Can do
          Here ’tis

After rest
Couple mountains
Tree tree tree

A pizza art
Ain’t that much fun
                    Rusted out

Wrist warp (gooble)
Trains around a fop
Inclemency is my

Ardence, twain on blue
Curlicue (bordering
Tumescent logicolloquy

Fritter
In as much as
Tippling in beehive

Throttle break-kneck
Copper wire (her lips
Bedevil

Forthwith
Yon kidding
Tell about see what

Linked reverses
Soap nationally
Verb fritters

Just to be talking
Yak butter idols
Melt into crowd

Fill in each crow
Syllables close for renovation
Phobia moda

Alon which twwitchhh
)Who?(
Surface under air

Each molarity obtains
Slurping gazebo(at)s
(Amy filters, John offs)

Mine cold and stony heart
Field marsh
Begs the governor

"I did not do it"
Nor foreswear
My cup to lids

Cut Outs

On fringe
Believe you me
Take it all in

Fashion

Absconds with lid
Over my dead body

Ur seasons ago

Big drop
Gum in many ways

Pintemento mori

Tracks effluvial tissue
Wasted in Wintry

A second 12
              Place ball

Make that throw

And then
And then

And then

This is
What

Made of of

Knotted by a Divine
Incognition of acute

Release

Gray plain

Unison
Rest of world

Iridescent quagmire holds
Feet to surfeit, pangs of
Blistering confines

Track big storm

Large HOWDY
Win da rain

            Flips
Like a (slike a)
   Girdle on an alligator

But wait

Uh-huh
Oh

(Griddle on cream cheeks)

Sis? Bob? Pops?
LOL-OLL-LLO

OK, knew what

Naa her off
Waffles waffling

Into the Bollywood moon
Gim me uh broken
Spear, dusty tear

Say name

Know something
The moon in Paris

Ssshhhimmmerrrrrs

In a black night
With golden edges

Eagles

Not sure
Telly Y

Veers to no one's quandary
Trip to fall

Equates jelly with juried

Orange pedestrian

Clamp dead to
Come to rye T

Square squirreled
In some dark whole

Flagrantly

Mais oui, buddy
Be the pal

Undermine message

In soda POP!
Like an earl in a snow blower
Filigreed to an inch of

Not sure
Dot blue dishing night

Sorry parking a lotto

Speedorama fluking
Finsters malevolence
Oxy, oxy, oxy

Clean rhapsoda

No 1 supposedly
Leggo lookalike

Where
Weights
Roll

And for a

Little while
Nice ouch

Sparing ((—
Quilts while Bayonne burns

Spittle by spit

Run tests

Sneaker chaperones
A little

Hideaway, slunk

(Fluts in an oak tent)
Secret even to herself

Getting late early

Double X street
Okay, what?

Nones & nuns

Forment ideality
(idiotically

Terriers in Paris

Major both side focus
To the righteous of

Minimum locution
Rounds out

Firefight

Butternut neigh tier

Heads per capita
Dwarts that gount

Bray, circumwrench, tookenize
Fairly amiable at times

With Georgian diction nipping

Nothing moves

Know something slices
By time begotten

Inalienable times
Inscribing hence

That came before

Winter cut up

Arrange til meat
Thumb bunt

Threaded in colored
Light, between

Avenues of furious

Fuck wads

People going insane
Flower bed Bettyboos

As I/you/they melt
(Are you there, Larry/Sally/Jill/Joe?)

On a wink and a

Vile tuna (verb)

Speed date weather's decor
Turn frequency tabla rasa

Vilnius, mon amour
Tattles its tale
Retail (retell) only

Cloud cozy rows

Borrow so told
S'mores

Engine set for overdrive
Surreptitious infatuation
Sunrise at point blank

Me not to come
Him lack mail she
That'd tell what'd

Or on again, off again . . .

Wends pens like hens
Cooped is the new coupé

Talk tutu green

Twinning keystones
Rufruf 2ndFamily story

I meant to tell you, I meant to tell you,
I meant to tell you,

I meant to tell you, I meant to tell you

Mean to me

What
Me fait mal, Johnny

All the way to the parked slot

Iowa Jima, Bugsy Siegel
(the whole *!>?**^! gang)

Twerky fall sky

(Last time I looked)

Listening Polaroids
Nods
(nods

Or else or
Else or

Ten Cents a Dance

No
Way
Out |
Where
(The)
Home
Fires
Fry
| Doesn't
Get
Bigger
[We]
Talk /
On
Phone
\ Makes
Sound
Evil
Needs
Get /
{Done}
Sedan
Bearing
+Straight+
Into
Compass
(Out)
Right
On
=Sidereal=
Fountain
[Purrs]
Compose
Mental
/ *Break
/ ^Pass
Quirks

Quake
Lick
(Lick)
Bygone
In
Error
Ear
{Car}
Writ |||
Across
Maybe
Maybe
| Never
Take
Left
(To)
Chance
Per
Tram ///
Per
[Far]
Rate
Strip ++
Adage
+(As)+
Broker
(Amiss)
Grit
Coffee
Newspaper
=DEMI=
Teeth
Keel
(Dead]
Body
In ++
Radiaor
Bag
Keep

(What?)
__Talking__
Park
(Pluck){{
Kiddee
Kar
With
Slelling
Nightmae
[ ]
OVERAGE
Legitimates
Famous
Chocolate
Shops
Sponging ///
Detention <<
Beside

Casserole
(Slots)
What
Is
This
::::: Threat
Shocking
Images
Blut
Après
Windows
Blow [{
In
Who }]
Third
World
Person
(Detonate)
Fun
Love

Dance
Allata ^^
Favors #
OK
Lightbulbs
%%%%
Honor
|At|
Call
Brick
Studio
:::::::::::

Sobriquet

for all that amounts

basic sobriety

Withstands

adjacent decent

quickens

visiting mic

unable tackle

inside selling it as though

m   issing

catch fall

what what what

I never hear you

even when I hear every other word

they had to save the village so they could

burn it later

as a soul is saved

so it can spend eternity in

a war zone

(unbless me mother for

I have not sinned)

skin and chop

run over cook and serve

live cousins slithering around

best eaten with finger icing

on the cake

back out on the road

(slurp)))))))}

is as as is as when is how but who is what or
fails the folk that tills the tears and mops
the rent as dry as bones as when is then and
now is not nor even such as is is as and as
is so and went unbars the if in stiff as. . . .

put up with

adorable moment Bulgaria

come tumbling down, reach out

one of my people detain people

on rooftops hearing and seeing and singing and sweeping

what's going on
plan

for inevitable shenanigans

wish I'd just dreamt that

(flushes)

AS IN

You were your moccasins and she'll wear hers

out

of the park a high fly by Masden listen to the

roar of fear, the silence of terror, the wayward

any time

No play around

old spare fenders cut up around grand

fold hands

fill in in between there

pretty good tea

no problemo

except when there was one

sails on the green beam

wakeful in sleep

(arrow, burnt, hiccup)

switches so fast it's like a Yukon tire on fire

may as well, can as well, get a hold of, dismiss without cause
frustrate mandate, defensive at 800 feet, blustering idiots,
salon talon, get with it (was it?), filigree insensate, clover

and the falling pilot

chopper hit

tiptoe flight path only too happy

overshadow

unplanned as planned

ascend escalater attack homeland

ringleader slips on finger

pretty scene in car

sure bet

fully falling, as planet

titillates

inchoate cohesion

Jody says

Whereupon floats until the isle of tug

Liberates location

(loquacity's amour) on the line

race car ashtray

(fate the thorn no man averts)

big willy car with hemi off white

just the hope of help or hint of hurt

restore the way

where possible and then some

large number that is exactly counting

eyed to an inch of mire

give tanks on tracks

(just not not now)

rare coin corners

Fly to outmoded centers

hold one in your hands

or, like they say, any way you can

——————-do————————-

~~~but donut don't but me no~~~
~~~

Breaking News

Day turns paragraph
Proxy comma sighs
Medical meadow A

Séance in triple meter
Dull determination hedge
On silicone arrivals

If you or loved one
Without you and no they
No this magneto

Tango goes by code name
Divine pairings: tea & . . .
Mango presto chaser (to go)

Pharmacy saveur
Right people connect
Enroll phone on over

A vast wish land called my
One step back, two steps back
Constancy, created in cascading

Not one step back
You bet, Joe
'Tother way

Invisibility, joined at the harp
Drop to phase
Adroit busybody busting

Let's make a party
Throw some these away
Missive home

One step in, two steps up
As go I go to where
I know not know

Oh, Brooklyn
Your Walt voice
For many kettles

Flagrantly alights to
Missing corners
Gust in, gust out

Earrings
Shedding and itching
You got it

Soaks earnings like your tired
& poor make way to err's
End in Thingamajig Mountains

Man like father
Naive you sound
Five years legit

Four paces onward, five stones across
Make grace a
Stone seal in a deep pit

Send back Detroit
Celebrate pure body fat once in a
Any lengths {go figure}

Doldrums mum the domicile
Erect in each detail
Mystery soaks up | | | | | | | | | | | | | | |

Here at local
Come on down world famous
Sleep nevermore

But quotheth knotty
Been then dared thwat
Out by the muddy, out by the muddy . . .

Too soon to say
More own tears
Memory clean fill

Against all cost of recompense
Cuts to the narrow
Allays what falls under care

Won't believe wha hoppen
Catch break
In advance of Aram

Withering, wondering, wondering
Fetch & recalibrate
Hand's breach in clutch of instant

No frill mudflats
How you doing, man
Candy here go

As in: doing done, done, done
As in: funds transfer aborted
As in: „,:.?p)*(67$}\{?/>,<∞¶§•¢≠≠

Awesome new plan in works
Works good as looks
Make believer out of believer

Five steps under, three hurtles upon
(Belief is neither bad or good
But the tide we swim with or against)

Isn't for you
To say the least turd
Why in the whorl

Spits and spats, grins and slaps
            A girl and boy and all between
Set out on the road to

        Nowhere fast
Lips first
        Before it's honey, nut

Gets by and then some taste
            After more turns less
Sugared into squalor's haze

        Life size cool enuf
What's crazy, always first time
        Level of clean

Makes calm as pantomime
        Of last week's rhyme
Silhouette racing ennui

        Signs all therefor
Don't think Why moi?
        What's the deal, bub

33 for 45, 78 for 92, 21 for zero
            Aligns with starlight ministry
(You can't even trust the trees)

        Open up
So finally, important conver orb
        Won't say, Sugar, wanna doc

1.e4 c5 2.c3 d5 3.exd5 Qxd5
            4.d4 Nf6 5.Nf3 Bg4 6.Be2 e6 7.h3 Bh5
8.0-0 Nc6 9.Be3 cxd4 10.cxd4 Bb4

        No more easy parts
Saith the Gunman, POW ERRRR
        Thought wanna get wanna wanna

None more than the giant, she said
Arrayed around the table like a
Like a like a like a like a like a . . .

Gonna get things done
Widely debunked outta flower beds
Let me ask about claims

Twittering on the verge of clips
Clumps, clubs, quells, curbs
Got to get, got to go to

Edge of sanity
No one else has seen
As I live and breeve

(Bereave): king to forked tongue
Rook to rook, castle to
Make-believe ballroom

Block Marty inizing
Bespoke gone rogue walk off
Pat the page where's doggie

(Breathe): lump it or lack it
Floweth the Golem
In the seams and whacks

After snowfall
Not an easy way carfare
Go to wardrobe

Five up, seven over, nine behind
As in: Where is the snowfall
Of tomorrow (who said that?)

Danton, he die
Ooo, son tone negligee
Shake docs to cores

Locks in a box: never bore!
In time takes nips
Coagulating in | | | | | | | | | | | |

Another reception not much room
Here comes some running back gamine
Threads evening's fiddling needles

Threnody of liquefaction (5 oz. servings)
Enables Mercator projections
Let's make, whaz tha'?, an intervention

Be surprised to see
Plate ready for dinner pictured
Can't sit back, no no no

Coagulating in, shake does to
Snowed under, care free
Spattering on verge of edge

Delayed backache
Mopes in sunlight
In yonder window

Masquerading constancy joined at
Pertinence shedding hearings
Believer levels beliefs

Ice coffee high blue
There's so many details get it right
Areas put stuff

Matters make us
Upended to a saw
Old one, tracked with clatter

Make back ones match
Not argue, good mood
Leave that up to you

How Come?

Ice flows
Seasons debrief
Lazy vicissitudes
Enrollment deadline
Sutures amend
All kids have dream
((Come haze, come sound))
Spuds ZOUNDS!!!!! a #
A million million million
Families really struggling
Tasting the dust
Celebrate your # moment
#as *soon >as %you ^can
Buttercup butter up
Ingrains sultry taverns
Jumping bean boredom
Cistern abuts solemn
Saved frown from
Overland mirroring
Drugs as cause of death
[#Drugs @ #causeofdeath]
Take that cat home
Or as far as the ear can bend
Before the fall falls
Swat sit
Augers all for
Perfect pj's
In the quiescent marrow
Good answer motivatation
Lingers as such in such
These R soma keys
Left on the back seat
Every breaking story angle
Ddeelliivveerrss iittss sswwaagg
Bygones gun sales loophole hooples
In the cool dunes of the dumbed
Mouth fresh and clean

Steel jaw for glass times
Local corn beef versions
Of versions of local beef porn
Walking syndrome
Denotes ecnoid fallacy
Desperate winter twigs
In set-piece locutions
Per profiteroles on parole
Quips splicing sorts
Clouds rolling all-sorts
In protean exclusion
The phone asking
What's the exception?
And baby makes 4
What the rue?
Sticks
'n' throwns

As You Know

Wishful clouds
Kind of affection
Scoop out night

Trespass against fortune
& traipse in

Wainscot

Such that I, a never sworn
Adventurer

First order
Most comfy world shoes

Drink ad verbalization last resort

Blood on ground
No pants no shirts

Baleful sweeps
Kills affectation
Scout around a bit

Incendiary machinations
On cutting room diorama
Hip to the long slog and short

Estuaries

The like

Break open agency

Handling kindling
{unrung}

Signalless lanes
Tomorrow's pre tense

Eggs

Over easy

Or detonate as readiness wearies into
Formula for exculpatory excavations

. . . on tempered shears of mock replay

Given all that we have, had, hid, sift, get, gorge, simmer

{Yokes}

Over hardier passes

tHan pUrcHaSe wIlL AlLoW

Tell your doc

Right for me

What about you, bud
Three finalists

Remove nightlight reel
Head of steam

Message spread around

Man to pick up

In graze sunlamp imbroglio
(like the man says)

Olympic gestation

))incriminates((

Absolute lesson in door jambs
say it, say it like I want to heave heard it

In bloke-baked positionality

Featuring a full run of flatirons

[ring]

(ring)

Not available
Shaken up
Watch hands here

Lighter stripes
Knock thru

Mom or mgr

Tight as the ground that roars its last

gummy gonna get you
honey on a fake flue
money owns a faint brew

"If such there breathe, go mark him well!"

So I arrived right on time and I told the manager I wanted to work only in the mornings that I had family problems I needed to take care of in the afternoons and I wanted to give my full attention to the job when I was on the job and she said it was not possible that she needed me full time and if I couldn't work full time then she would have to let me go. Let me go where, I thought.

Uh oh

Uh oh

Oh, uh oh

Nah oh

¶§∞¢£

¡™¶§∞¢£

¡≠```~~~

≤≥˜µ≈≈≈≈

Nu?

Chilled in gust
Where went, shall go

Oh, no

Top Down

Lone wolf actor
Lots of counter parts
Victim forms
Death warmed over
You look like
Just been activated
If you can tell
Lots of counter parts
Or you take the pulse
A catch by the book
Sifts in place
Just been activated
Thrush sip of vaporous
Lone wolf actor
Throng elevates
Paragraph day turns
Proxy comma sighs
Heard before after
You look like
Listen to band aid
Victim forms
Graze medical meadow
If you can tell
More sigh wildflowers
On way upstate
Death warmed over
Made from scratch
Or you take the pulse
Get the jimmy
Sways about 10 feet
Not in here anyway
Proxy comma sighs
Get the lift now
Paragraph day turns
I found out too early
Graze medical meadow
Shifts your focus

Medical meadow A
Boss says, The fuck out
Up and walking
Weather's family recipe
In a gesture
Foot down
Life as before
Is never after
Lump sum payout
Goes by the board
Still there's time
Or was or will be
Goes by the board
Up and Walking
As I never said it
Shifts your focus
Or maybe I didn't
The fuck out
Up a way and back
In a gesture
Pretty important
What'shisname
Sitting here thinking
What'shisname
Weather bring up
Soooooo . . . this is . . .
That's right
Shifts your focus
Hey, man, lookit out
But still none of
Question of phrasing
Still there's time
Whenever you call
Is never after
I've just got to say
The fuck out
Here's the plan
I never cared that much
The fuck out

In a gesture
Don't get me started
Or maybe I didn't
I've got to say
Sold for more
Out of the blue
Is never after
Cute threads
Empty locks
A while back phrases
The news cycle
Lump lump
(New ad)
Smoke ring
Dad's hometown
Very thin craziness
Oh, you know
Out of the news
Where to go
How to deal with
Control possible
One hundred percent flesh
All told, or much of it
Like the dinosaurs
That incredible moment
Before it all collapses
How to deal with it
Very thin craziness
I'd just bet you wouldn't
Last person to get out of bed
The moment's past
The bullet ricocheted
Out of the primordial ooze
Did they land yet?
Did you land yet?
One hundred percent flesh
Out of the blue
Notice how hazy
Check your shellac at the door

Notice how hazy
Morgue spins
So it is
Key tooken
History maketh not
Catcheth fly balls
Oh shit, well . . .
Cheesy birthday big mo
More people
Can just kiss my ass
(Glare)
Mind what?
Nary hearing
Me ask you this
Family there
Money's curbside door
Brings dog
Hand a kleenex
Leave on table, please
Warden warden
Outer too blue
Even in tune
And you were never that
Focussed on the other side
This makes this
A mean percentage
Goes below the depth
No wonder
Given all that's unspoken
Me ask you this
Given all that's unspoken
Check the specs at the door
A mean percentage
Even out of tune
Worth a ton or price out
Market forces, says who?
Smoke ring to boot
Fifty more beside
Careless? That's a

Even losing the tune
Given all that's unspoken
Takes my breath
Reach higher
That's the scam
The dream blah blah
Fa la la la la &c
Is still in business
While it lasts
Are voting
No wonder
Running for our face
Get in the way again
Even out of tune
A little money
Reach higher
Discuss the how
Are voting
New procedures
Slotted for release
Best or 4s
No wonder
Fresh modern lookee
Mnd what?
Here real time
I put it together
Moral numerals
Fend for themselves
All the fucken time
Buried with the dog
That's so weird
I scarcely was up
Pump erl
Flat out in the open
Curves and wimples
Duplicate repetition
Good to awk
Mines the word
File for a minute

I put it together
From afar
Notice the hazard
Continue to demand
Entrance directions
Right and rung
Thoughtful gliding into
Rigid decomposition
Weighing in
Doesn't go well
Lake search
Will last for days
The mom said
Blah blah
No answers there
Risk to public
On mental health
Because off ear
Global Persephone
Business before
Busy tone
This latest survey
The fuckit the matter
The saith wealthy
Green with idols
Use copper tone
Then some slide
Days in hours
Flooded gates annul
Motion delay
Visits score
Sweats a lot
Layered in templates
Flowering simulation
Norms all blocked
Weighing by the pound
Simply as such
Sort after plenty
Fled in show

Sobering derealization
Ambassador of stilt
Searching sucker pop
Done gone home
Thoughtful gliding into
Simply as such
Notice the hazard
Stoop to touch
Discuss the how
Then some slide
Grade makes tip
(Be emptying)
Mines the word
(Be enjoying)
Days in hours
(Be filing)
(Be untying)
Even out of tune
To do so
From afar
Not true
While it lasts
A foot before
Take my breath
Hey, man, look
Up in smoke
Die drop
Down the scape
Flitting furrowed wrench
Simply as such
Torques even slap
(Be situating)
(Be incurring)
Stone mason rap
(Not done)
As far as will lets
Up in smoke
Days on first
Then slides

(Grinding every dollar)
Near to natural
Slowly warms the pot
They kill him
Need the money
One foot up

Still Life with Thought

Sits
quite close
mends
when needed
What
is
amazing
meaningful
deflects
call to other
Venuses, desperate
trial arrangement
curries
dial in
drill down
what the fuck
anytime like
wax walk
sleep off
Night knife edge
dial in
drill down
what the fuck
anytime like
wax walk
sleep off
Night knife edge
FIDGETS
in place like a Mounty
facing heart wind
DEVIOUS
arrival forges appetite
(call to same)
. . . name game, onanistic imagining
frequent miasmic episodes, furtive
hurt, improbable gait . . .
logrolling

off the bench
can't stan it
Gaining ground
questions
Opening doors and arms
unspoken truth
K O front runner
snapshot tempera mint
HABITATATAT
liberalized osmosis
until the jam is stuck
right in the middle of end
(so she says)
brokering a highball for ascent
GIVEN
runs out of dough, no bread
sayonara, in plaid
Go fast and turn
puke glitter
your father's name
your mother's legacy
Got grapes
White guy in white suit
lotta watta
here on top of fire
put bed back up
driveaway
Make what's need is
FORLORN
as aggravator battles aggravator
primacy locks wings
in tread, when boxes
Floats where no man
nor girl
(WAIT)
Grievance in spades
of sumac and shale
drives body deep in brine
Woolgather memory

disappearing vowels
snoods for all
good Orlean years
the which way moonlight
(I know)
I never had it made
Ride across the BRIDGE
Hold me for the Moe
twill text is time
and quill be scum
(with barrels of rum)
sup not, sweet friend
stay not, sweet fear
BILIOUS
& say again:
to waver and to tarry
And while the rest
age denim
dial 0
don't like this bags
if don't pretty old
unfeet purpose
half advance mirror
'tother stal 50/50
on mark as set
beguiles the throw
and seeming aims
dethrone
THROTTLE
bushed traits undergo
intransient taint
gurgles a little
chthonic lethargy
soap bubble auras
it's not about
Actual designers
a lilt ad before internet
all orig docs forgiving experience
30 mpg

heights quest
frip moment
a completely diff major
{dream cascade}
not just a car
de jure
How'd I et this dis thisease
Wednesday
gonna make me some moo
Come Fall
in:re:ex:un:sur:
proofs the rube
a cathedral
bouncing
22 seconds per second per second
[sic]
[———-]
I aimed for the best words in the best order but ended up
on a range miles from Dodge without even a rope to burn

tulips are better than hum

(you can't say that again:
it's the wrong number all over again)
Thread lives

Another Level, for Sure

Certificate of authenticity
Please show
What's the win

Gains in the belfry
Lionizes insurgent foretaste
Even before dawn

Check it out
Make money off of
The Baby Cheeseburger

And then the chase
Around the spot
Of ceaseless churning

Sorta otherwise
Differing betweens
Rubbings

Askance glances
Afford asteroid interrogative
Only time can tell

Lips R seals
A lot on plate
Beat, no skis

Deftly, prickly
Weighted with wear
Torn from

Gone line
Or call loon C
Re arch spaces

Inspecting notions
Thorn in the alley
Weigh to boot

That said, donation
Long history
Appearances about

Notation, delay
(Say: hey!, ho!, hah!)
Littler by littler

Take come backs
Fall to shoulders
Preach eats

Bending round bumps
Only to reappear
In crooned tapers

Take come backs
Fall to shoulders
Preach eats

Fleece in wary
Tropes, crusted by
Sudden, glide

Jerk head
Deep tendon
Way dodo

Elope at set
Done the tub
Obbligato to a moonbeam

Partner nods
Some guy

If do this

And then not
Or not the same way
Or never as I expect

Knew
Dime
Enters phone

Falls to the walls
Feeling bad, feeling
Badly, alert to

Smoke ring
Pick up
Is at you?

Not any more
Feeling iffy
Taffy, sundry

Button button
Lovely dollars orso
Sightseeing any

Witch way: have
broom, will travail
(Into the garden

Hear birds sing
All that shit
Match head hotter than

A hornet's quest)
Fomenting fidgeting
Ballerinas in Macon

Nope
Take look around
Mess up

Delta or dilemma
(See nothing, say
Whatever . . .)

Sip notes
Clip ping ping
Much stock in ballet

Smooths radio fever
Clover mannerisms
Detonate denotate

Used to used to
Word in edgewise
Sun downsize

Spiraling in place
Jumps over cube
Mannerisms a must

Go Tell Aunt Rhody

You're the kind of person
'ld burn the forest down
'cause got pricked by a thorn.

Nice, huh,
woman here to see you
Y
have get inside dope
slap shit
outta really am

So I could get you the same
exact screw but silver.

Any good
Check service
lean back
got and buy
Turns toward
Somewhattheysaid
off chest
Manages to steer
road invisible
tries new tires
febrile imbecile
(to say the least)
doses
dese dems
over phone
with is
That's right
in hollywood of all places
spoilt
on foot
baklava
M itchy

no dice, no play
(duh, dough . . . you dig)

TRIPLY BORNE
FATAL ARREST
GRAB-BAG TUESDAY

over even before you arrived on the scene
with your tune in your hat
chip chipchip chip
heavier rains
power outages
record highs
first two payments
favorite pesos
expresso
teleprompting the blind
go there quick
fear in mouth
cascading islands
just off there
worried honey
it's wetland all the way to
longplaying operator
2 words
Thought you were gonna
celery the car
What time?
Breast and thigh glimpsoids
It is to us a liver
ivy frown
pork orchid verandah
gee whiz smoothies

You've received this poem because of your interest in Panacea Productions. If you wish to be removed from this list please send us an email so we can include your verified address on the list we sell to Internet marketers.

Breaking News

So sure
(A number of signs)
A bowl of stew
Alley entrance
Okay, who?
(Who know no)
Where, elegant
Exit to stubbled
Allegiance, tight-fit
Occupancy as long
As trade perspires
The beat oop
(Been jail)
Down hall
Pause spooks
Lookee loo
A number of signs
(Fair solace)
Alley entrance
Grades denuded
(Exit to snubbed)
As adds article sac
Occupancy as long
Embed rejected
Who know now
Filter, fits, lumpee
(So sore)
Straddles atlases
Mark green
(Lush lanes)
A long listerine
Fends accomplice across
Slender hand
(One month later)
(Too frightened)
Light voice match
Cleanses hurt temporarily

Finger nails
Ugh
(Chaser)
Pledges somnambulant vigilance
Hammer to toe
(Grace to be)
First start talking
Alien ascents
Versus
(Subcutaneous smoke)
Great hits
Bounce back
Debate about future
Reverses Orderliness
Write number down
Feign acknowledgement
(Straddle atlas)
Seat witnesses
First start talking
Then some
(Great hits)
By guess feel
Alien Ascnet
Alternating circuit
Bounce back
(Grace to have)
Feh
Sum accords
Come down
Knows no
Perk or less
(Fare solace)
Hear them now
(Arsenic and old farce)
Head bob
(Herculean rampart)
Want to look like
Breaks even
When it jerks

(Now and against)
It's that close
(Hair wave)
Just next to
English corners
(Hammer tone)
Triple plague on
Morningish swipes
A dark suit
On the job
Or isthmus suite
Piss away police
Mind saying
Needsome
Money broil
Try deny
A child anymore
Bribery devotee
Undo freight
Take up quaint
Comb caution
Eye form agency
Ill got groans
(Try when high)
The meme to extreme
Mind bending
(Child no more)
Rated by weight
Riverball mudslide
Or is this sweet
Needling the haystack
(Annealed more like it)
Eye for age
Quaint racket
(If you can find it)
Such bleats as smoke
Crinkly apologies
(Who bear what may)
Book habit

Ingratiates
Bite research
(Doubly spoiled)
Anything else skulk
Lash as clip
Stinky insight
Just just
Wane for want
Before dawn de jure
I tangle
Trow hands up
(Sips, chaps lips)
Frop brack (non PC)
Ooo E
Agrange in despoil mode
Lie behind the lie
Sleeps all ours
Forget yours
Trenchant, ineradicate
(Nomenclature)
Pours stymied
(If you can't)
Ear for error
Noodling half-grains
Brick path
Combs down
Shovel view chips
Perks or gets
Somebody boo
Broke event
Once slept
Where it lurks
Phone hoo
Wear wades
You can tell me
(Was that closed?)
Quoth the venn
Too tight
(Door slams)

Grab bag
Arrival signage
Holding hat
Head moves
Sacral irrelevance
Side to side to side
(Joined at hurt)
De pend ing
Grills in state
Really funny
(Quit looking)
Like hat
Play joke hook
(Heavy breathing)
On all
(Molding fat)
Cat runs wild
Next week
Nod jam
The idea had come
(Red groove)
Suppose
Those faze
Martini in hand
Feel out
(Touch light)
Wherefrom voce
(Once kept)
Indie sugar iteration
Bromides for the tone
Bicycle drums inside me
Focus, Focus, Focus
Comes the dragon
As long as up there
A dumb question
Slipping grocery
Sounds good
Thinking wrong
Turn key

In curly locks
Space related don'ts
Bulbs included
Keen teardrop lights
Adrool
Sunset adobe
Drink it in
Or spoon whiskey
Into life's pores
Twenty to two 'll get
Five to three, seven
To pour, over
Hard, stirred then
Shook, Coast, Cater
Alarming rendition
Permanent Overdrive
(Crossing guard very cross)
Whimsy close to wail
I go as I
Stay as I
Piss as I
Wonder as I
Flexed shiv (shiver)
Atoodle, atoodaly toodle
On a pale blue night
Navigation system failed

Liquid Amino

down by choir
delivers motion
not sure where
street sweeps
dogs on roof
Woofwoof
laments larcenous
other pockets
get 'em! get 'em!
wait now to do
[crunch]
more than who have
what, which, how
zero by zero time
for every dime I
every dollar count
butt line
no fear wear gear
where no woman
glance above the icepack
in little dotage
playaing record heat
kids' touch
can do it (donut)
thump by thumb
oasis as backbeat
take me to your
lava lampedosa
grilled answerlings
(sur bun)
yooouse to be, now aamm
in tree canopy
under slow mo
(all those things)
energy coming from
don't turn our . . .
whatya, whale of a

aside
I do what I done, stuck in
what's going on here
(killer couple)
wrong up in smoke, folks
till the crack sounds its
sentience
neither there nor anywhere
such as
what is OK
kinda absolutely blah
indication of tracking
indication of backtracking
indication of stalling
comes to idea of
people travel
far and away morph
(soda jerking for a lark
find myself in the park
way down below the . . .)
lost tic
snow toc
batteries whirr out
or into
broad coven of pale expanse
astride
50/50 off off
(immune boost action)
phone smart [home]
alert to fall in premium
gone by of dead end
got to buy
negative review weather
enjoy X-related pins
hahaha super happy with 3 p's
ends up over dial
return to flick
(sedate arms arm not)
but aroma yo

[breathe the breath]
oooo eeee oooooo
and just like [this]
shooting the breeze
and then it's none
heartfelt ovation [(family night)]
just about perfect this fall
when turn did said leaves
sworn to be yet lorn
where quench to fold
on backs of strangers came to test
too fast too rapid fire
known in Italian
[agent where all had seen]
match wits wit
flare for same
if flame names
more than flickering
perfectly clipped
nail in, nail out
ergonomically so [fund]
that you ax
the or is it such
can even make
or soak
in a world
live (c)overage
unnerstan what am saying
in prey some, lost 'em
squired
describe cell
quality of life
magic pill
one life to limit
with mule and pale
[sequence abort]
this holiday
you need answers
no obbligato pineapple

a caper a day
clacks with alien parameters
keep your park [intubation]
above sea level
shut work
permafrost
lily-leopard in 3.2 phasing
jumpropes around sash
(in all this time . . .)
tone so angry
quit in 3 months
mental health problems
arrayed around a [ ]
lumps in the load
blister mock mood
week sick continue
up the gut skied
throw get to
[*show down*]
neither / where / nor / where
ever … severe … weatherer …
[(rack it up)]
cue white clouds
building rails grate
—|||||||—
seals shmiels
on a day dress
digressing like mandolins
praying for brunch
(|/|/|)
help more difference people
afta dat cot up wit leven
iffa go back justi fie li
snare, where, care, tare . . .
naked when busted
out of loop
chew grill make data soup
(||)
bowl of goodness mako phtt

mon favori tingling
shhhhhischhhhhh
in blotto delectus
unmoored by mob
winter's meows
^^^^^^^^^
kitchen's dinner thesis
eggs overage
when flat floats & tarts imbibe
igggggly pigggly poppp
shames the carapace
leg warmers why not
twinkie infrastructure's longueur
scratch back from tooth and cole slaw clawses
even I ingest with caution
(certain that each fleck)
filter of abiding ghostliness
where police did flake >>>
each and every ring around the mood
sweltering miamiish articles gone thataway
(twat, thwat, htwat)
gilding gullabi
quacks in middle distance

How Now

1.
In media's res
Venus and her flytraps
Wrap herselves round
Vainglorious chaise
A life that saves
Whole kit and poodle
Immediate reign
Shuts the fly's wrap
In lieu of sand
Candle the candor
Well's lilt and strew
Incongruous haze
Decline switchbacks
Wander into late stores

2.

Pertain to worried countenance
Afloat among routed slur
Strange things are hop ging
Winters retorna due days
Slips happen, ways crowd
Endemic ort thaws *übermensch*
Begin a root beer
With a fine old whatchamacallit
Sus in sus out, anxious to
Avoid even the slightest hint of
All right   Let's go
Let off
locomotivelocomotivelocomotive
            Vests

3.
Model As and Model Ts
Second private thoughts
Dash by like figures at sea
Model As and Model Ts
Public demons' guilty pleasure
Middle position kicking and screening
Second private thought
Such that prisoners sometimes see
Sit doe, GG
What's wrong with moi
MM common everso
Bar yuck, yo!
Dash by like figures at sea
Such that prisoners sometimes see

4.
Even as
Weights, or
Sorry, pal
Great holiday gift
Even as
Sorry, pal
Really love it
Can't cut bread
Weights, or
Not today
Really loved it
Given all that
A nervous
Homage ingredients

5.
Beefy num num
Return to offering
Summer deftly
Okay to to to to
Somebody with
A small wrist
Gets into deep
Not saying how
Can wear it
Not small even
Winter's bowler spares
Epoxy clouds slash
Erases cultural meme
Frozen on the square

6.
Aquatint
Overflow
It's true
Add to
Bequeathed
Sift
Dot
Directed
Mandate tour
Go between
Increment
Bond
Fast
Friendly

7.
Back from Canada
Right date code found
(I don't know where that is
Or how they went there)
Know who's going
With meme
Dedicated to the one
Wears her hair in a bun
Talk down
Walk back
Dial down
Fuck off
You you you you
You you you you

8.

A flame, roused from insatiable manner
Immediately takes to thread, supple
Rights when stop by cop
Grandpa look a that
Delete a draft, investment
Sweats out on ordinance
Swift untruth denies
Dismantle the setup
Cars twice time wind down
Streetwise chips dip pity
The same, indifferent to a tug
Escape delay at such peril pose, strums
Ear to thumb to nose to breast
Notes not this vapor, scum adroit

9.

Try remember a person
From then (sonal) aw gee
Fends for the flip he can
Makes off with flight's risks
No idea chickens
Beyond a reasonable daub
And that's not for me to
Say, what's, whether, why
Shortly before it dawn
Boot leg with rocky spur
To act action wit dimmer
Douse with have a gas
Fear (own) shadows
Strike dusk to dust

10.
Lunatic fringe bores hole
Air leaks from neighborhood
To me the big question
New voters come out
Insulation of longing for
Exit the faceless froth
A muscle I forget flex just
Before doorway little ago
Arrondissements circle the wagons
Patient trial for pagans
Release brute uncertainly
Going about your business
Enter endless
No word yet

11.
Enter endless
No word yet
Forbidden just
Turn right after
Froze maniacs
An elsewhere lullish
Finessing the weary
Prisms of antiquarian
Bigger writing (hand)
Glimpse new phase
Take a corner
Ghost flames
As a habit worn
In and about the face

12.
How much for it?
Is this and this the same as that and that?
Leaves on road
Small ball weather
On which I preyed one time
Sufficient to traipse
Thoughts turn to
Belly very same
Left hidden in store
Selfsame reproach
Malarkey by the barrel
Fools interned in blend
Congenial exchange
Rest forehead

13.
Congenial exchange
Rest forehead
Leaves on road
Thoughts turn to
Play some crystal ball
With no parentheses
Wash over in silence
Fish out of water
Hedge sparrows
Spaces in out spaces
Avoid disappointment
And future regret (regret)
(Thoughts burn through)
(Space in space out)

14.

Crash course makes the hay shine
Cubic system's default
Squirrelly end long branch
Next tree, which
Devours its kin much as
Sloth devotes itself to hope
Clover fresh sweetness
Emotion's dawdling dawn
Zeros in on Claymation
Fuddle of all get out
Brine for the buck, twixt
Image for image for image
Uh, where was I
Then again, who isn't

FPO

you
slip
fast
under
terrace
raise
bar
(quilt)
capture
beware
a
swag
with
remote
pick
a
line
take
out
ad
re
pre
position
para
tundra
await
call
of
landfill
destined
for
arc
sate
saturate
provincial
mimicry
endures

long
abutment
pace
counter
grace
insolvent
time
to
step
up
in
complete
wind
handling
flag
down
tacit
unnerstan
ning
pining
for
place
(slapped)
onto
magic
mirror
(I
told
you
as
much!)
rates
ºº∞@#≠
wing
spawn
thirs
(thuck)
SSPPPIIIIFFFFF
adjuncted

landmine
(crow)
thother
seen
to
be
felt
and
cherish
skinny
former
legs
(aaggg!)
torrents
as
genie
bombastic
iridescence
(irritants)
SPLAT!
(accrue)
(anoints)
parlor
valence

Wow Factor

Reading around
Can't grasp
Gray chest hair

Rusts salt
Mine gratis
Opens sieve to

On tonight
Like or not
Hubbub wheelies

I got to say
Mills for thrift
Don't buy no

Duck out
Walk like a
You know what

Greasers in pantsuits
Alloy with irrepressible
Simpler than Shinola

And shit from
Weather closed in
Can hear nowadays

Anyway you take the check
I'll wait outside
In the pouring soot

Walk this back
But then that's what
Satisfying mono keys

Too Late for Tears

Shipshape, not on your life, not if I gave you
A whack. It's not the intent it's the effect
Matters. For so long been down here I hardly
Know what is going on in your planet.
Screen in bones
wan noon
small and almost
Toy-like rain
adjusted like like like like
WiZRD sow replicated QZZIClllty
Indentured as the plow make plaint
deterred sombulance
Turn and look
look-see tooken
unhook
not too not too
Wheon foresay wit's uncumborium hup ith melt
On fronze as whaze infends gallant inbroke, cavate
Jocase entound, surt vehemous glot, finswot okque
Inject or vent to truss its oat in tert ovay, ovay
Worry come around
thought so so
drop off another swallow
allow for temp changes
talkee kid to chili
glip, gloop, glup
And away the ships took her, to the fardy coasts
Slimback, royal floo, abysmal
$ jam, gustacious debacle, florance fire
(>>>>>sssshhh)
Can stew be OK
wintersky day
whiskey call
the (of) I d A
What say
And it's down by the greenwood side-o
Down by, thrupp the mooze

Jilly come quick, come fat, come stout
All alone and so lonely
Ton of bucks
like these guys
just inside tree line
cell tell

Thin Dim

One hung low
One dim sum
Tree addiction as it is

Placed in a jar
Rumpled in sway
Still steals moment

A birch beer
Birchbark whatnot
So da weather

Inclement, frayed
Woods that lost bearings
Jilted steps in pour

A bridge one night
Red eye brake light
Tap tap smoothie

Beep beep beep
Sure set at filigree
Totes nest of lilt

In error
Drag mistakes
More dead heat

Than live splutters
Going around in spheres
When not at the

Fork full
Teeth bite salad
Mash up, swallow

Intricate bracing
To full-scale bric-a-brac
Phillip scrooge diver

Crystal message chandelier
Gotta go here
That's great

Finesse as predictable
Uptake on the downs
Sure sure sure

She's a new
Now girl
Knew it, too

Birth weight transglobal
Globular, gustation
Interred in interim

This thought
These
Those

Which, was
Gap
None too few

Gone
Frown
Right up

Estuary state
Singular worries
Tingling

Grouchy faces
Is it just me
Or is it that you

Quaking on the outside
Waking on the inside
Taking in between

Silent Seething

Every once in a while. The je ne sais quoi (fr.). Tears into the open air, a biplane without a rut. Look deep within the deep-end heart. Fixation, floatation, amendment: so much spit in a whirlpool. Winter turns, to go out the door, sleet, take yon nob and turn more so, is it, clockish, seconds only for woof roof. Torched by agreeable surface, mystic runways cavort to tonier inlets, tucked away in pockets of persimmon, sibilance, gator acrobatics. Meow, saith the beloved, for the endith is Edith fenderith wailing in Obama earth sans jack Wheeling West Virginia all roadie WWVA transmitting lu lu lu transliterations total svelte. Really did, that I can't and won't and wouldn't for a word of stealth become agent of your impeccable surfeit, shady days after all's said. Well, my hear, where is the t, the only one you're ever gonna, or is that going to, or too, gonna needles, needless, to sew, say. Agent regains foment, forlorn in treed recollective, sturdier, fence-facing, then the go around again and the blistering cold. Never saw standby workers on site (not add value). On the air! See some polls, twitching, say again (not rhetoric) join live. Hearing phases of the moonless night as trains haze border regrets and fleeting decompensation ennobles its ministries. Along the way tuning across the country the best place, it's easy, to suppose put a comma here, okay, make a success of it come as a no-one surprise, you cannot talk what you have in mind without national authority fat. Rats! I just want to make it to the sign, all this fake rain, neon warnings flashing in my cranium, solitary company, the whole schmear. I'm old enough to remember a little bit slow the outsider. Slept in the over those years. And under, the number, too. Bluing in every shade of green, like the old man says, when you can get him to talk so you can hear him. Shld be space. And then not. Complete pizza a quick slice gulp. Down to the drain in flashes, like the pulsar gun in the glove. A minaret of chips shape of the wind heart of a lion. Desiderata on the wall, leaking into the cavities. Not we, even more slowly, but you. Instant gall at lift, scrum in the barber chair, hot towel and all.

Just Weeks Ago

Mercury delivers chrome
Outline wheel well
No thank you coffee

Adjacent to cement
Winds article to spend
What not never toss

National debt can do
Bad news on roads
Colossal ass pain

Wends formula for canasta
Ables in abler out
Suits us

Makes think about
Crave it
A point in balls out

Famously
Surreptious amen
Accurately encounters

Country by country
Bird lands hard wire
Where to heard where

Flat and pierced
Ogles barometer
As is no yesterday

Dash off some sleep
Make sure certain later
So happens fine fine

Gaunt wents
Intrepid tempts
Sibilant sours

Pick up plane
Ticket from floor
Two foot plant plant

Juggles reminded silently
Change in hole
Holler past decide

What you guys doing
Closer closer, hmm
Familiar what's called

Echo without a glance
Forward epigone gone rogue
That maddens the hours

Wanna pick up
Weekend
Taste for your yo self

In the sweater-cold mooring
Leaves swept in wind
Adroit as all get gone

One thing though
Real ending unhappy
Hear him what?

Leap to sputter, gaze gone dry
Foregone conclusions remanded
Wending way nowhere

What's new for news
Today's weather worth
Song lines to dotted fold

Life raft overboard
Hit ground crawling
Fact to fate

Ice coffee
Breakfast sandwich
Anytime soon

Or so they say, said, sold
Now or ever hold your pace
Backpack to the wind

Live oak mood
We the
Words ball bounce

Swift courtiers, dude!
For a
Orbs alt. bound

Good feeling
About a drive
No car

Securing surety
Bonds that disgrace
Just sky, stone, steel

Love these things
Base on data
FIFO per scent orf

Charms, chums, chimps
Chattering to the mud
On/off/off/off/or

Dream frags
Tonight's select-o-matic
Sleepy goody

Gots gotta get God
Stream-o-phagic choir
Down by the haze . . .

Everything happ(y)ens
Out of nowhere
That's all (you) need

In slow love, love I
Queens and Kings love
Way into Far Rockaway . . .

Rather pleasant day
Recent history with season
Positively Homeric

And when say hop, hope!
And when say mop, nope!
Such makes for hay

Play drive, stop short
Other guy inside
Can't find the drawer

Parts against liquid lure

Deafens modern pole

Snow comfort
Right light, just
Centering bowl

Swing, sprang, Detroit!
Oh my aching fibula!
And then on to what . . .

It's the 1950s
After dark
Go to party

Flames all about me
Or is just another song
On the transistor radio

Smiling chemicals
The real me
Hold that thought

Smiling chemicals
The real me
Hold that thought

White Lightning

Like some Chiliastic piano player
Humming along to show tunes
While fixing the plumbing
I wend my way, dodging bullets

In the souvenir store by my house.

FITTED TO FIND

Gun control (as in)

immunity from give and go

PLATES Á GO GO
follow us ghost

(so when you say so say so)

life change therefor

I've still to
snag a tickee el.

Super monger

insinuating stalks

billets for who knows how much
(for a song)

A/C on
[check!]
Stuck
[check!]
Oh, well
(can marry marry marry O!)
A/C off
[like I said]

Oh, well

As frequent as a run up a millstone

Surge in rent

Long coat old man

always walk daily

eaten present paticiple

spend day

try to buy I'm trying to sell

gradation
excision
annulment
ramify
coat-check

so fly in the
wizard of

Signs are pointing

Hotdog bungees
coastal flooding a problem
Full moon this weekend
meet under clockwise
wear winter weather
should too

Weather these coals as you weather treasure
Take it to the store to buy some clothes
Go to the mine to fund the measures

Big boy words one pants a time fail state
Invasive microbe as tailor's suite (give back)

Feels like 13 the coming snow talking with Dad
Grows ungainly in forensic wild near shit storm
Sound uphill pair a pants cloud shadow

Inseam with sullen occupy

Slow chocolate movement

Pretty tuff words print in so many words
like a lion with horns
take out the hammer and sickle
(*sip slowly*)
beard
(*eviscerate hold*)
work, argument, no
yawn as in make-believe
Bring out young people
(*throttle*)
the process. Look, Ma,
no hands
stems, eyes, arms, neck, back
of the man who walked on the water
awhile
Hoping credibility psh over idge
Schools close hundred yar go
hi, fly hi
dip toe in revenue stream

songbird hooks
RADIATE
steam-fitter put on flak jack
(given all that's not worked in)
simpering succulent
go for the frozen fruit
bottled up in some

melt locker

time'll keep silent, you can bet on that . . .

Dashboard

Eyes close
Around an inkling
Page numeral

Driving an outie

By filling station
When I had my fill

Already

Dawn's departed
Over that warehouse

From now on
Everything (I mean)
Flush left

Where was (I)

Pacing to the right
Pacing to what's left

Inasmuch as you could ever

Solo slope beat curb
In the dust storm of the bent

Sit on steps
Breath catches up

Another feet

Gels dust to restore
Still quiet beat

Raises

Opulent trumpets
On call for mourning

Passes by

Morning ear
Close to hour

Ask for order

Steam inside bamboo
Care for beer
Make thing right

Leftovers

Honey – Lace – Willow
Beats in a series
Way too sly for
Oboe – Medley – Thisle

Glides sum for magic
Aging deportment filibusters

This L
Man with funny neck
Cleans curb
Next next door
Ramp stroll
Ambling toddler
Wanderer remembersish

Formica-like swelling

Abysmal breakage
Starts day with fetch
"Darn cold in there holes"
Autoanimation trivets (so say)

Shoot

Do your checks
(Vacant puddle)
Flip script
(As when I say stop)
No bargain
(Says the other guy)
Soda mostly soda
(Basest motif)
Numbers mostly matching
(Graciously rude)
Body pretty good
(If you say so)
Killer base
(As in run fast)
Here's the deal

If you can't stand the heat
& then it was as if
Sulky sort of sifted

Movie inhabitant
Seated page front
Heady lines
Of those plans
What's realistic
Corridors
No changelings
Building coalitions in DC
Reach out
Other side gosh darn

A hornet's nest
Of hornets nests —
Watch the baboon &
Raccoon play house
In the master's mansion

Goodbye to all that
Went by and what does
Will, has, can, and may
Rest is never more than
A momentary stare
Away from the glare

You think it's plastic
But then remember
You're not first person
Even if it feels like it

Build mountain
Three lines
Tree no fire
Nice lite
Twill

O, come on!
The snow is a wet blanket
Mocking human unkindness
Even saints would swear

Trigger Warnings

Say it's so
Even though
It's not

Crispy clouds
Booked Friday
Done things

Beat the drum
Until the bleed
Makes sunshine

Bowl click
Door shuts
Leave room

That's Why

Catch up on
Pity pattie w/bun
Don't mind ME!
I juz got there
Mission scratched
On a paper balloon
Flip side of
Slouch
Syrupy suction
Game day minutes
Watch less
Watch off
U can
Just imagine
URself
Wasted/wasting
Soder pooped
As in slider, just
Make it smack!
Dab in pain(t)
New according to
Arbor lights
On lawn in lawn
Drawn. Still pointillism
Box box re
Mark words
Fret. Fret. Stet.
Amazing lace, how . . .
As in Amazon lutes
Trip over tip
(¶) (§) (∞)
Direct image
Made of stone
That reminds
Mountain refit
Two a day eye
Ask about

Whatever the . . .
Inclement charge
Overestimate visage
x > x< + = <>
Silent testimony to
Visceral decline
Body parts one
And one and one
Tools around
Lotsa stuff
Hiya
Quickie resulks
Bottom line
Play (nano ice) now
Various grunts (vague)
Shortchanges ayahuasca
Boot to hip, gind
Fecundated fry-mason
GGGGOOOODDD
Knows no limit
Secretly snorts whiteout
In flush moments
Flesh is measure
Everything's video
Music to
Lyric irises (complete)
Sprinkling of trees
Dots for cloudy
Contrail hills
In good old rays
From light years beyond
All's misunderstanding
As bliss or miss
Functions to the left of us
Fictions to the right
Inward pierces
Sorta aces
Do C how so
Pet crow

Don't show the card
Grannyless plot thins
Shoes remove
Behoove our grave menace
Sipppping stripes
In gainly odes
Fraggle'll tie you in dots
Jetstream of goat milk
Haze (portment counts)
Voice thrown
Crate talks
Into the pot
Same sentence
Coming out rabbit ears
Up on yonder ruff
Doe a deck a betcha
Bores its premise
Until you can't bear it
Flummox will melt
As leave chum
Beside monitor
Occam's eclectic shave
Motorizes remorse
Life lock card trick
Door falls off fridge
This can't be
Happening to {preposition}
Somebody else
Barnfind morning
For which wince
Zeros globe
Freight in absolute
Reclaims impermanence
Overboard all over again
Power stations
Second interview
What's it out
PB and door jamb
Or sorta E smiling

In head
Low hanging fruit
Swacks the thwaite
Given times given =
Obligation tithed
To the dock with
Thick roads, welter
Of comeuppance
Filter shot, man whole
Woman fissure, plate
Dissects decease
Can't say
I blame
No blam
An election who-knows
A lotta people felt
IOU
In reference to [deleted]
Marred by beckon
So very slowly
Even a mother would deny
Being being what it was
Equal time blasted
Outta the pink
Fuck-that master
Made of stone
Blue blues
The point
Next line
Looks wordish
In a mama's boy way
Or swirlish, time
Tells just very
Quiet, along the river
Dreamy goons in
Fat suits
Zut alors
These are my people
Who are Natalie

Doorway from
The back (off)
Kitchen table recap
Amenable to stasis
But not static
As if the chassis
Dislodge the metaphysic
In aerobic tussle with
Cho-cho ch'baby
I cling to (clink to)
Put a tail on
The very idea
Therein lies a
Rice above details
Elastic words inscribe
Brim insignia
Foaming filigrees
I hate to remember
Jimmy, Jimmy, Jimmy
Sunset on latent
Get-to-the bottom
Silk febricity
Revision weather
Snow temp globe
First thought pest
Pressed dough pesto
Re-bad rimesicles
Imminent mirrors
Seriously, I meant
Gig of microsecond
Sedated auto fill
(Think I can, think I can)
In red velvet
Pppopppsssiiickkkklllle
Having a ball
Ricochet off
2nd person singular
Search, train
Complex world

When
Still in rain
Off it went
Goes bats for
Suits, pants, shirts
Zeno better price
Zoe worsted
Dog stops
In a jam
Sweet tweets
Slippers slip
Hole hole up
Lick look
Never know which way
Who's who
Where's which
Govern in a thing
So motley with
Sure, sure, sure
High in nite sky
Rainy nite in Queensland
Ball is star
Bring own wall
Weepy and gabby
Skin pumping moisturizers
Depending on motivation
To deprive of
To fortify with
Gyp, slip, glurp
"I" in trance to
So long, soldier!
Morning pronouns
Personal preps
Severing situations
Like a big pizza pie
Empty indisposed
Hole plug with nickel
Ever at disposal
Grates pavement under

Degree of filament
Thrusts microphone
Into rabble, kismet
On Sunset & Divine
Every rake a cure
Forgot milk
Think THE
Wind need dough
Pitching mustard fun
Cap tiptoe tip
Mandala umbrellas
Beast for all got out
Shucka shimmy schlep
For all the world
Down windwood way
Oceans apart and yet
Peas in the rough
To which tip hat
Year ago (this time)
No memory of (actual)
Terrible (dreams)
Heads upstairs
Close to ceiling
On the painting
Drives it to the id
Just don't make me
Suborn to penury
Like my nickel's a dime
(Flippant Procrustean orifice)
Fiddles while (static)
Proof relieve pain
Tell the doc
Freeze away
Hey, Doc, gotta tell
Onboard spending money
Want more proof
(Whiff of the money)
Soot to suit toute suite
Bien, alors, Fibonacci

(You mean "be in")
Stuff that stuff's made of
(Transversal segment interrupt)
Oh for the old digs
Limit dominoes
Airily encucumbered
Vastating unalloyed
Multi isms
Avec eau
Veranda rail
Right past my occipital
Contraption: depend on
Whomever wonders faster
(Base violin, you dog!)
O me o my o mayo
Oof salad white down

Transcendental Mediation

Such
Says
Sway
Mote
Cleaves
By
Sibilant
Loss
Grates
Premise
Intimate
Moment
Maybe
Last
Who
Cares
Who
Slam
Dank
Bend
Bout
Surry
Wake
Rend
Motion
Cops
Pleat
Pucker
Triply
Islet
In
Reproduce
Bay
Peoria
Worn
Snow
Or

No
Winter
Wonder
Who
Wend
Nounish
If
Er
Gee
Sputttter
Coasts
An
Orangutan
Tan
Grilled
Disses
O
Sword's
Slow
Decant
Load
Binary
Imbecile
Who's
Right
What's
Going
On
Gingham
Am
Dream
Ick
Replica
Liquid
Splatter
Forbids
Search
Where
Gets

Got
Gust
Sum
Prickles
Bromide
Replication
As
As
Retreat
As
In
As
Fudge
Drip
Dust
For
Who's
Right
What's
Going
On
Gingham
Am
Dream
Ick
Replica
Liquid
Booms
Insigniac
Lilt
Obeys
Programmed
Viaduct
All
Wizened
Stardust
Decamps
Instigation
Launches

Loaches
Lift
Like
Lurch
Lulls
Graded
Simmer
Into
The
Bloodstream
Making
Light
Thou
Sand
Nickoff
Clouds
Dogs
Shed
Floors
Thinks
Uneeda
Fluke
(Raise)
(Ripple)
(Root)
Gone
By
As
Like
As
Made
To
Swap
(Sit)
(Salve)
(Imbricate)
Total
Minimum
Ovation

Sizzles
Pieces
O'
Mind
An
Old
House
Friend
Deal
In
Lead
Y
You
Came
Back
A
Man
Like
U
A
Place
Like
This
Y
Bother
Descend
Tripe
Play
Fix
Element
Jabbers
Milky
Motion
Shirt
Shucks
Shunned
Tempest
So
I

Crest
Ze
Quake
A
An
And
Andalusian
Delirium
Pot
Slump
Gets
Better
And
Better
Un
Reason
Able
Search
And
Seizure
Blood
Sample
Comma
Please
Un
Tainted
By
Hum
Ans
Melody
Signatures
Sit
Ting
In
And
Lear
Ning
Swain
Gins

Management
Highcr
Slap
Goats
Liquor
Precondition
Solicitude
Wanes
Florid
Intemperance
Alloys
Hot
Fatals
Feral
Encumbrance
Lettered
Loops
First
Take
A
Shower
B
The
Future
CC
Happy
Happy
High
Per
Form
Ants
Gear
4
Great
ED
Planner
Panic
Wades
Emotional

Whip
God's
Whorl
Hotfoots
Egress
(SLAP!)
(CRASH!)
(STOP!)
Mates
A
Manic
Auto
Barb
Inscrutable
Lush
Stores
Clutch
Evasion
Liquor's
(SCREAM!)
As
When
In
Alms
Sets
Mission
Slide

Worth Getting Out

Most peaceful
Most at home
Now 20 miles
Isn't a murder
This
is
an
execution
In
Until
Isn't
Done
Sort out plans
Made to say
Flips on you
Major fuck up
Back to square
Like I say
Slips outta my hands
Shatters on the ground
Pieces a puzzle now
Still in play
Few more openings
Mind the shot
Tears out of park
Waving arms

Two Cents Plain

I always say if you can't go the distance

bunt

Fact of animal life

Homer invectus, homo neurotic,
half-bred *intellectiones*

If you can't stand the incense
Open the window

Like a pizza clothing
Debbie
Golden harried
Not big, too
Like a bigass bag
Pun dittoes' dahlias
Happening
new
now
Actually will C 2 ants

formidable

In elevations well below sea weed
Encounters its own encounter

fleck, insoluble, tokenization

As with all flies, unswattet or
techtonic
for the third strike
followed by a deflated spare
(story of my life)

Indian head diameter
measured in pixelations

Silvery mental
lure
fishing for some
something
(Weather update)
Yes
Yes there are
There are too many
Forgotten face travel

(ba-na-na-nas)
(ç∫√ç˜ç∫≈∫˜˜µ˜)
[÷≤µµ∫˜µ√˜∫ç≈∫Ω∫]

Flea in the cr0wd is a c0w0rd
(Say it again in §∞¶§¢¶§¢)
fl0w rate remains static
abn0rm0l hibernation level
let's up the ante

X
MARKS
THE
SPOUT

Semantic
Spillage

It looks timeless
Let's do it
Kickass power
Best
towing
two-ing

wasn't for wires
episode left

THE tired iron you left in Memphis
now's in Minneapolis
(a swallow away from Capistrano)

People with brash horses shouldn't stow thrones.

{VOID}

{PUNCH HERE JUDY}

Panting hair
one leg
wanna touch
same same
Nother
Comb over
one foot
deep
In heirs

Bloom by starlight
Not likely

Such as
Such that
Such like
Such song

greedy little puppets

over lickity splat . . .

We gotta go thru this
a gain and again
bippity-bop

Shmoo-like clouds
Down into muck
Am not are too
meet with person

or person will look you up and then it's
just, jeeze, a slow gin fizz and a walk to
the laundry on a cold and tawny night, sleeping
by the balustrades, banking left to throttle
the keel, aching for the end of ache

If
U
Think
Haul
End
Up
Flip
Pin
Have
Some,
To
Say
Gunna
Float
Fundament
As
In
Sew
For
Sup
Slaw
Makes
Ends
Meant

sill on floating slide

In or out
Next
Time
U
Pay
Yee

Giddy as in giddy up, amigo
Flash of musk perfume
Golden buffer turned to truffle

Inapt

(note to: ¬˚∆˙©ƒ∂ß)

1/2
to close
It's com
plicated
pelicano
Bread w/ margin
fear what whim repairs
(Jeeze)
(shhhhhh-ooo-tttt-iiiii-nnnn-ggg d'breeze)
paired with lemon meringue
Fortune to have landed
Foursquare pajama patsy

Hoo
did what
ca
to us (tous)
Homey
Rippley wall
Believe it's a
maybe
You're
(tous) themselves

ricochet

follow the flounce
gee hah gee hah
straight to voice mail
(the caliber of heresy is
a chicken in jam)

No roads
in
between
(in)
B cleansed
This dress
in
an opine
neon
Cowly hideous

Hideaway, by the farmer's cheese

•stipulate force of evil
•cancellation denied
•offput numbler

(seriously, I . . .)

crank

Enabled by Plymouth
(constabulated oasis)

versts
Leaps and boundaries made
Once again
Never again
Wake up
Feeling great
Check out

Zone in

Bilk bate

Vote take

Worsted suits and frapped flounces

Jelly on a roll

outflanks mercurial

Every

1

goes B 4

Colorful Rod Co N

O Can A DUH

No 1

to talk 2

Pic up

(hello)

Pho N

(lil-lil-lilit)

SOCKET BRACE

scourge (of/the/

Slim picking

Derange wars

(tell 'em it's all over the papers)

BITE the wand in the

(paleocene)

Think of nothing

2 say

No

Exceptions

Wind

picks up after

Itself

Day One

Still time
Stand still
Some asks

Brays welcome
Opening rejection
Spills decay

Voice with teardrops
Sigh sightings
Sightseeing pretzels

Similar sprawl
Contains fragrance
Fragrant doldrum

X pect B surpriZ
Razzle drizzL
Smell smOke

Okay loooka
Forensic pajamas
Silence magic spore

Selfie stick silhouette
Have what to hide
What see must take

Or then again no
Not now granted
Stick and bows

Raise with rags
Local details
Perfect person

Decalcitrant huff
And all
Even so, so

What hear
I.d. Hours
PO now closed

Regularly
Can uh can uh
Meals of malt

Cool
But not 2
40s

- —- - — - —-
—- - — —- - - -
- - ——- - - - -

Up as 1
2 say so
Do say $

Lops to side
Days go drip
Lands the fuck

Tidy cats
Number on screen
Straight talk overages

Semblance in stir
Chunk MAX slink
Every other over

OTRC side boobs
Prescribe in class
Important side effects

Wear with all
Degrades
Inaction tantamount

Prices compare clouds
Red brick bird shadows
Screen fits in a year

Loop de looping
Dodges shadows
Shipwreck manifest

What U make
Of what thin read
U doing wha wha

Sail without sun
Detainer r r r r
All loopholes

Mist steps
Writ to perform
Contrary to all writ

And then annul
Gust frays balance
Hope smogs theft

Red yellow sky blue
Shampoo ready
In data record 2

Along the perimeter
Gurgle in hand
Th-th-th-www-aaa-ckckck-iii-nnn-ggg

Wldn't it be great
Certain nutrients
Schedule echo demo

Slams on the backpedal
Somnolescent cluster
[Place widget here]

What's singing
A boo out
Call it LUV UV

Rue the neighs of Antoine
Cruel quilt stuffer
I is a same

Doinel bon dust mote
Big must-have weather
It's auction time step

Walkaway wear
Dominates the ruse
Oh Jimmy, Jinny, Jenny . . .

Speak another mind
Pronounce left words right
Voices never waves

Intransigent in inconsequence
Fiat forgoing forfeit
Place slams all ministry

Ice in fence
Tornado comes
Blow town

Its its its its its
Sounds segment
Arctic arrest roaring

Another chance
Of rain, wear
Ball go to homage

Outing in frame
Wear for whimsy
Rend Cove, Amen!

Wonder of the modern
Wonder world
Not cloudy

Yet, but then
Just you wander
Three feet to the

Traffic
Models with eyesight
Eyebrow cloverleaves

Lazy until the phrase
Where the monster
Disappears in a puff

Look down on traffic
Point to elephant
Sounds familiar, mmm

That was said
Don't bother now
Selves inchoate

And talking
Look ahead terror
Police search for police

Overrun metier
Sings the chorister
[yeah yeah yeah yeah]

Is this
Very here
Y home

Sort a sort of
Solve of frisson
Crazy glue of my heart

Big disconnect
Friendly face
Yah!, what a face

Burns like salve
Opposites binge
Who might let slip

Clip lead in with
Win wind
In whole sentences

Agromancy falls away
Titular apostasy
Grips under the radar

Nice sound
Door open
Hang up

Quells arrears
Breast pocket brace
As in hidden premonitions

World left aflame
U wld pro-pose?
Keep safe USA

Smell Test

Toady's of the regime
Frog goes plop

Cylinder empathizes
Fools in polka dot.

Hello, stranger
Pains tiki bar unfolds

Got out of there
But gone nowhere

Wider bluer
Wirey rakest

Storm drain failure
Hideout mislaid

Afternoon's details
Neighbors intervene

Slipped calibration
Delays dalliance

To be honest
I'm in shock

Whist for the grill
No money down

Are wives
Trouble A coming

Derides lisped radiance
Akin to mishmash

What do you do
To stop

Bets on the bottom
Swain could float

Listen to himself
This guys a senator

Anchorage sale
Transient arcade

As line
Opens cloud book

Fluctuant adherence
Cart with no art

Wrist's elbow
Lift off

As been as
~~~~~~~~~~
~~~~~~~~~~

Cherry Blossoms on Schuylkill

Geese nibble grass
Sun swolles sense
Congeals at evanescing sentience

Blabber wall
Intense with proximity
Always, duh, something

Concrete melts in air
Sloops of exile
Drifting into port

Heel of shoe
Bag hands
Call comes

Lame proviso
Sucker punch salvo
Spilled beans with twist

Unbelievable!
Alive and ivy well
1st Amendment

Phhhhhhhhhhhhh
OMG0OMG0OMG
See funk think honk

Easy release weather
Bikini wax clouds
Loan some artiste

Palookaville slugger
Right in the swain of tain
Arguably . . .

GIMME
Cell phone
QUIK

Sluice, shroop, schlusch
Fused with
Interspecies buck

Coming off (scary)
As as as as as
The bad year (really scary)

Stares right into my eyes
& she says, she really does
I couldn't believe it . . .

And she's driving now
Forget U
Head in bag

Hardly even worth mentions
(Slow ascent is same as)
Forebear is foresworn

Down runway
Best high school hair
Fake blood

Girds the grid
Juice smokin' and all
Sorting the way

Drip drip drip drp drip
Teenageize getting together
A lotta dish elations

Swooply, is that it?
Egrets, too, just over there
Beside the police line

All, eternal
Morning cut loose
Look around new guise

Sunday Kind of Love

picks
up
where
thought
trails
ask
you
guys
doors
close
wavy
palms
a
nice
leg
a
plan
bags
snoop
I'd
been
meaning
slakes
thirst
tars
drift
cuppa
did
thanks
later
solve
ball
with
hat
word
eating
moment

cooking
garb
laments
total
phase
in
as
in
eh
in
for
buzz
breadth
wizened
soar
slate
in
just
just
mini
utes
re
nts
k
lll
ump
or
jammed
in
joyance
beamed
as
wack
O
manic
lisp
lilts
lore
fff

the
cat
canyon
woody
afternoon
no
names
please
abhor
I
I
I
jaundice
which
make
that
which
cult
drop
something
true
what
they
say
forward
deploy
eyes
that
that
that
same
thing
(boring)
true
(boring)
fallacy
upon
the
pond

of
uneven
char
stuck
in
same
old
r
u
t
t
t
then
chill
in
(hear)
defoliate
all
getting
used
used
to
how
do
what
light
in
every
rumor
piece
miss
(ing)
ing
ghh
snip
at
catch
breeze
floats

face
fares
snap
aptitude
alarms
in
bilbo
snore
time
on
a
ship
binds
mind
to
touch
meet
all
commas
woods
in
words
bottom
pal
line
me
luv
dogwhistle
invisible
ink
wink
media
meet
clock
sock
dock
flop
frock
fickle

dedee
dumsy
'n'
dumsier
cleanse
wends
when
change
tone
ends
some
play
pities
tons
fare
quaint
makes
orbi
, , ,
grasp
set
cull
troom
don't
B
annoying
cloud
alloy
hills
to
pine
atone
the
somebody
else
confuse
for
me
U

this
hiss
aways
U
art
got
some
on
art
walls
basic
intro
version
can
calm
claim
frets
to
tatter
frrrrsss
grizzle
inter
^^^^^
dope, , ,
plan
creeps
, want
a
way
to
give
back
slice
a
sluice
(suede)
carapacio
vision
cuts

swealth
goinggg
gimps
feets
not
to
get
too
kicky
wits
not
gotten
SWAT!
UGH!
er
thrown
withers
o
ver
couch
po
ta
to
got
out
take
pix
borders
gleam
on
err
ides
fired
sum's
,
sorn
,
silo,
hey!

either
ear
bother
life
behind
the
life
behind
OFFSHORE
salient
entire
vamp
it
make
it
gawk
several
um
soot
gh
can
have
mo
tooth
ah
so
ingenuosity
velcro
sunset
bitter
coupons
day
mind
blind
Bilbo
ecnoid
housepaint
simmer
maybe

you
got
this
from
dad's
that
snare
bums
omniant
inrage
incroyable!
(feint)
reruns
BEEN
SAYING
headlines
brick
absorb
no
no
touch
BEEN
SAYING
all
backing
away
good
describe
up
to
devoters
as
as
as
as
astride
par
for
a

uh
an
ah
o
o
or
silkenly
soak
(sloppy)
Decatur
in
the
course
an
effect
what
a
though
state
decorate
coral
stare
find
out
cloud
cover
bread
broke
hew
glue
X
actly
WHAWHA
eye
know
daft
bars
hurts
snakes

meandering
bee
you'd
snap
hags
pan
an
egg
knit
sand
harms
wait
clap
oars
gee
who
takes
trap
slit
here
oop
pricks
hair
thru
aah
lot
total
dead
face
,
you
know
nice
be
indoors
speak
ruff
a
row

nd
da
etch
Calvinates
expectation's
silt
subrocka
envision
sleepy
(}
:::::::::::::::
(gilt
guilt)
fountains
stray
electrons
mosquito
bone
word
to
wise
(find
new
roads)
change
(some)
change
(some)
fade
into
charm
(strum)
crazed
impossible
reams
to
instance
(score)
down

runway
cuppa
coffee
reach
back
,
moron
REAL
WORLD
WHAT
THEY
MEAN
winner
take
all
states
of
Mindy
WE
ALL
GOT
BOSSES
frozen
stare
innuendo
attends
inoperable
bleep
times
smoke
rings
lassoing
experience
clept
severance
holds
fire
call
the

NOW
in
flaunt
of
bay
circle
in
redeye
stick
a
round
circle
in
redeye
stick
a
round
crushes
rote
wears
then
beam
=
sort
bane
groping
spat
wh-wh
vexation
slumpers
muster
a
static
dreams
make
make
dreams
tunnel
light

800
or
so
set
wind
jams
bird
beep
(ugh)
, SIS,
the
doors
loose
cares
make
static
slumber
groping
bane
rotes
crushed
wind
picking
up
up
after
it
it
sleeve
left
shelf
self
windows
blow
off
homes
power
outages
falling

debris
cupulah
uh
run
din
stoner
mescal
electric
splay
futons
start
with
giveaway
fast
moving
sky
quept
khool
cuz
ache
hems
heart
not
a
bad
place
to
be
from
or
travel
from
where
here
curses
there
whatever
bunts
it

isn't
that
interesting
underpolls
eternity
not
a
good
sign
mind
if
ask
mind
couldn't
help
thinking
call
now
brain
splints
to
I
recollects
border
saturation
and
leafiness
by
by
(struts)
egret
flies
over
vamp
nothing
feels
quiet
like
take

U
R
PK
feel
me
what
me
know
vast
pleasure
across
today's
today
eye
on
clouds
ears
grounded
sootly
sound
rolls
tuttering
throng
gains
begun
pillories
ocean's
copious
mmmuuurrrkkk
§S§s§s§S
(the)
boyler
fie
foe
ffffuuummm
air
chillier
pressure
drop

(song)
don't
stow
stones
stow
don't
(song)
drop
pressure
chill
airs
depend
solo
rippling
if
not
for
high
negatives
low
forgives
the
fear
just
simply
this
room
with
third
eye
floor
spammed
ingredients
garner
fools
like
no
get
out

while
you
just
swear
Jesus!
if
I
if
I
if
I
ready
to
travel
sorta
showers
buds
budding
just
got
interesting
sortassear
you
flooding
duds
ust
ot
ear
uds
iff
I'd
bungling
o!
sorta
fudge
ooding
sting
got
what

if
the
was
a
place
why
wait
to
meet
someone
great
drink
chase
stan
the
thought
donut
ate
an
imals
call
bottom
line
numb
brrrrr
when
U
join
today
join
today
member
one
set
dogs
beautiful
piece
dead
kid

gun
go
got
gumption
flipped
fur
flume
interregnum
mundi
moody
switch
’n’
bate
cleanse
entropy
of
dreams
rec-
re-
a-
tion
funds
distraction
debate
socialism
of
the
helicopter
culled
keepsakes
girl
bring
sheet
stovepipe
info
handspring
bedsprings
look
at

map
move
forward
what
ill
tell
M
rain
begins
face
opening
day
bunting
brows
my
want
my
entropy
my
exclusion
my
saucepan
my
ineptitude
my
mince
my
fare
my
way
my
gotcha

Rehome

Party-free hands
You talk about
So much of this divide

Like old times
Flickering around
Lost ones

Smoky cloudy
Killer imitation
Watchful waiting

You talk about
Lost ones
Smoky cloudy

If it were not for . . .
Hand wringing
Chance to leapfrog

Still
Feels
Better

Echoes congeal
Metallic meadow unwinds
Sullen aire

One day
Write article
About THE A

Nested in an arboretum
Particle rhizomics
Male pattern blindness

Snow show
Crime scene
Who body

Lacquering the lake
Like a lackey in pinstripes
O buoy O buoy O buoy!

Lyrics come across
Fourth floor window
Early spring screen

You say, say
You go, go
You hear, here

Today's H2O
Xtra delicious
Great tttaste

Moldering memory
Sucking deceit
From despair

Train kinda stoppp
Harsh thud
Say as follows

Not pop vote (tied)
45 RPM big hole
This week 1st Xs

I coulda, wanna
Beanbag in pajamama
O say O saw O sag

"Trenton makes
The World Takes"
Always in blur

Vote value
Nice weather
Nice U Cing

Hush hard
Ollows az saws
Memes, molds, screams

Access road
Tsunami bring latest
Thank U 4 x

Bloated somnambulation
(Sommelier, screwdriver)
Boards the bus . . .

On the black
At the knees
Wind picks up

You walk about
Gauze of the heart
Heatstuck mannequin

Comb scene
Brush with danger
Bloom back day

As in as sin assassin
Blown away or blow back
Just in time

Find out
Lot a people car
Feel futurely

Under the guise uh
So soon to be mistake
(Alonzo)

Head turns
Seasonal all lights
Welling woW

Fooling me once
Spooling me twice
(Long, long @&c)

Heart organize
Diff walks
Ta do 2nd

Yeah whence
Garden ho
Spilling the idea of the beans

Heavy air
Days in recent years
Literal towns

Turns head
Light seasoning
As in as in

Candied daylight
From where clear
Can't be bull rushes

On the bum
Dated peregrinations
Pumped in testimony

Folks poke
Good call
Soooie

Entrancement checked
Foresworn by
Autochthonous mediation

Another chance of rain
But . . . little bird
Do your little dance

Or else I'll
You'll, wheel
That how till

Skunk whiff
Hello, neighbor
How'd your day

Beeswax in a bonnet
Quilted in all get out
Catapult, Klpetobongo

Loud crack
Here's George
Which George

Then gets got
Gates waste
Where in the world

Answers don't have
Do job great
Confide kids

Jimminy-come-lately
And all that tessellation
Aboard ship to

Cork cussing
Sect for nut
Bowls fuse

Chopped Liver

Meander in method

Swarm as motive

floatation, floatation, floatation
inculllllccclllllackkks

So, we too must change

Running to LA CA
Anyways grain of truth

Bad ones

rrrrroooooaaaarrrr

gibble de gobble
Throat hard

trellissimo fulsome ho!

Shush me up

Step on massage
Hard time speak pain

BOINGGGggggg

(ardour
flakes)

thoughtIcouldthoughtIcouldthoughtIcouldthoughtIco
uldthoughtIcouldthoughtIcouldthoughtIcouldthought
IcouldthoughtIcouldthoughtIcouldthoughtIcouldthou

Nestling over

[∞∞∞∞∞∞∞∞]

We R human bean
We R the countries
Of war of war a crydayday
I forgot
I look
Like this

n then n for n why n care n sift n spoke n
spool n dent n core n seam n search n fend
n toward n get n slit n gape n crack n

Big splash
Strange beast
Ant emerge

Lay on thicke

Wildering bell wetter
(whad u seh?)
flounce
Gurgling giggles &
FLAT OUT DENIAL
From outskirts
how cld this this B
Shaping up
RETURN TIX

4 more ears

ego's egoless ego
florid opportunity strikes out
Sherpa come hither and thence
to bet / Tibet
OUT OF A RIDDLE
senselessly lacking

Call comes.   In
Scales
Anytime soon

All right.   Unleavened windows
Weather the ticket
Gotta fire thicket mysef

throttled in thicket
think it
as rule is a toothless token
say you bite
but never prevaricate
muscling micro incunabulas
(septic phylogeny)
two and three and . . .

Beyond the (sea) press area
Arm re (call) coil
Like rif(f)le
Observe a touching

ringaroundaroseypocketfullofposing
over to 'ip z then when?'
(Sylvan dictation)
as I twarp marmalade torp

Spring smell
(Counterpain)
Contrail asymptote
(Split check's in the)
Clean light
(O'Grady insists)
Surferized memories
(I'll be watching you)
Revoib
(Over my latent amnesia)
Jamb over to floradoradora
(And jumps on sloop, sails to . . .)

Supreme diction

Eye poo
(tell me one more time)
we'll
(I gotta go)
be
(as in)
speaking
(can't be)
mean
(flippant betrayal)
by
(hope for no lesssss)
that
(surely/ surly)
We think
(In the bank)
The difference
(biracial hum)
Bank on cloud banks
(did I ever tell you)
in
(Secrocracy)
the
(“”“”“”“”“”“)
sense
(salience)
that
(slo mo : also sprach)
Isn't
(0h ya$)
it
(n0 g0)
strange
(Spezza florinide)

Tomato abyss
Race

over
Tree day 3 day fish
Take pole
Neeeeeeed
something great
to (verb) happen
Lobster abyss
wad a way
twenter D world
Stoop
Old one wears out
As seen on TV

or off
Raiders of Tossed Lark
direct keychain to
all acrumble amounts to
visible hawks
I guess I
table inconclusion
for
traipse through the vale of cumuppence

A foot is afoot
(*still starts the stain*)
Err on the of side
(ddddddd . . .)
Fire elbows
Light up exiles
(to wit TO WHAT to where?)
Map outlines
(Gen-you-ine lather)
Ah, meatloaf
Mon favori
(Mmmmmm)
By the cucumbers
I slept
(Air out)
Many dogs

Later and the
(the the the the)
genuflecting at remorse
Cuddling

Back-to-back fastballs
Evening works a walk
There's an old sayong
gotta piece
big out
stick around
Coming back on choo-choo
breaking point
Undone late
Lake like
Upside down coke
& go for
Constabulary inoculation
Immediate go-to, has-been,
get-from, gee-fritz
okay-let-'er
As inside the dome all you see
Is a vast hollowness, deeper than
Grand Canyon but on speed
Like a four-flush in the corroborator
Until I unplugged from all the weed-
Whacking elation and settled out
With the barkeep, oh when was that?

The mood
Like a plank in the air
What like
Sausage and donuts
Candy candy
Crush
Heartache and marzipan
Endeavoria
(Sleek like a pinched panther)
To be done has

No where in sight
Even in our
(Nocturnal)
Special country
Truckers by day
Sleepwakers in between
New day
(Say!)
PB & J
Chk point Charlot
(As cold as the war was was . . .)

Finger
In air
On the scale
Etch in stoned
Like all of us
Day to today
See the rain pass

Friendlier than a bumper
Cold as eel
Dead as dawn
Encased in glass

Create moments
Toothpick
Stand under canopy
    Magic mome
There's a music
    Veddy veddy

Not apples to apples
But rush to rust
Filigree to Whooping catch
Pillage to time out
Way out to just over there
Gorilla to not ever

and then went down to the basement
by stair
& with heavy heart . . .
See something
huh?
Say something
huh?
Hang time
you bet your life!

Larned skill
(No water in the water tank)
Inside comes
Last step (eyes)
Not apples to apples
huh?
Applies to apps
(Laying down of arms)
While the
July is July
huh? huh? huh?

Rust clouds
Settle along A-frames
Prop up
Birdsong scaffold
[Pilfers among]
A lot of pitches
You say to yourself
Fly in
Fly out
No cents
All right
It's theirs
If you got your . . .
DNA in stool
Shit to lab
White coat

{Alone among the birches}
BOING bird
System rig
Shut the fuck up
ACROSS AMERICA

                                        Derides
        Hoopla
                              According to reliable
Pattern recognition hardware

Here in Detroit
Whoop
Heart like bird
Still hopping
Roof brass edge measure
Tell U wot
Spit #
Dint kill 2 baad
Whooo knows
The right people
Person name
Jones Jones
OR WHAT
Dirt clods at cars

Amber disguise
Disquiets meagerer measures
Merger alone abides
Or withers
On your word alone
Figuring quiescent mosaics
Parked a block behind
A facade that is the realer
Thing, deposed for an
Hour only to return
Like the wrested, sweet
Songs filling the air

Fuller brush legs
You familiar look
And that fine, mmm

Temptation's sneaker
Throw a fits good
They condo it

What it

Future regret mist
Stir fries fee's friends
23 pairs
Possible daylight

Alone along
                                sappier
   hubbub
               then the return
Bounce
                                quits in sight of
      stand, tilt, jacket, thrace

"I mend a quest with vacant
snare of kettle fish and lucid
dawning, quickly to tar, quelled
in jointed store, as finer as
the top too top of pinion made."

Bad guys, OUT!

Nice.   shot
Legal deep dig
                                          Can
cashmere bouquet

or er or er or er or er
or er or er or er or er
or er or er or er or er

or er or er or er or er
indubitably incontrovertible

but
that
said
Spine momentum in Said
Going into New York
EXIT POLLING
ever
the
less
There are levers
Spoiler magic numeral
The delegate map
A wild ride
Spilling over into
everywhere said nowhere heard
ver / sad / ut / at / ess
ing / aid / xi / eg / ap

Selfless itself
Soulless in soul
Soundless with sound
Penniless in penury
Careless as care
Hopeless in hope
Fearless for fear
Precarious in premonition

Nothing but new born
Shoulda phone
No one home

Fire Lit

I cash clothes
A lotta respect
Come together
Good at oppo
See by nanny is shame
Go by real close
No aim no Fred
Crash course

99¢ Dreams

In the park there is an avuncular pigeon that I like to talk to. On the stool or off the stool I am the same guys. The lard is in the cupboard, the cupboard in on the porch, the porch in the garage, the garage is in the outside, the outside is on the, the edge is at the brink of ambiance. Meatloaf pantheon did you know special weather formula, something kind of intriguing entrepreneurship, spells. Ones of the same mistakes provide mystic veal across the face it only aye aye cap showing us, the royal wee wee, the way way into a hearth of parkness remember me to ole Greylock, good buddy, mon pal, aireodrome. Slumping. There was the quays all along the flashback, camcorder to my irresistible utopias that bomb out like bird feeders when the dope is cast. Slantwise. Whispering to command intention, bunt on homeground, bray at corner. I come here unarmed but full o jitters. It's a killer app / I'll tell you that. Two dogs hold the relish.
How nice.
Look back.
Take out on.

Whoa!

If it works
(Fat chance)
With the dinner
(Take a leak)
Couple pickles

(Out to supper)
Baked potato
(On rye)
Heat's on
(If you say so)

But it's spring
(Land of licorice)
Subtler stun
(Grabs the beacon)
Soonestest splendor

Heavy Lift

while
doing
this

on
other
hand

not
be
annoying

call
give
break

this
while
doing

annoying
be
not

break
give
call

foreign
heist
delay

make
ruminative
blush

Extra Eye Sets

Who's ready
Day One
Dated   Discussed

Dirt clods at cars

So Joe
Stumbling
Clobber

Tell me where it went wrong
Or we
Or who

          Simply

The hours, whose, where
          Multiplies by a thousand
Touch ground to simple

Shapes, tones, sores

What is the problem
With Michael Jackson

Extraneous

Put my head in the grinder but no thought came out.

Better grieve

than be aggrieved, lest the

wait of mystery crush

the tangible impermanence of the present.

Kisses paint corners

Hole array of everything

Almost a tie an exact

Using a lot

These issue Pivot tone

Skies not cloudy

All day allatime Yes it is

Buddy battery

West tear on legend

Get together

Sno globe friendlies

In love by umbras

1. Sent from ignobility
2. Stratosphere
3. Get grapes
4. It's extraneous only insofar as I want it to be
5. Make it look more messy
4. Relevance is determined by genre
4. I BREAK FOR SEAGULLS
7. A ring around a rosy is just a fall guy.

"I'm thinking of buying a radio. Which make do you think is best?"

Odor air cool

Saw out of sight seeing

See ya ingot

Music, Martinis, and Memories

gimme, gimme, gimme

said the stork to the python

crrruuuusssstttttt

in the margarine of the dorsal finger

Creature from Mambo
Jack the Soda Jerk
Hold the Ice

what'd you do

for as row is

greatgreat cloud
greater eat

breeeeeeeeeeze

yesterday's saaaaaaame

but is it
beauty's game aspect

No idea what's doing
do something

else

wise

Memories Are Made of This

Things

Like chop suey on Seventh Avenue

faded marks on hushed slips

centuries of

So-called so-scaled so-led

It's what we do

Paperwork

decades of unrest

Morning mouth

Or otherwise

sanctatifities

Garrulous at first . . .

(decade's cadence)

ffffooorrrrmms

s*i^ab%l#

o≈†poß†

berry vocal locale

These Eaves

count
digits

hands of extremists
same
time
same

station
Less one

Unknown Unknown

Tell me again
Like I never heard it
Spell it out

        sums up
        sumptuous

Like I

Spiky intressed
Look anecdotally

What Is Given

Spiky intressed
Look anecdotally
Tell me again
Like I fell into a spoon
Or pong or pun or
Spill the beans, can
What you cannot
Take the day to
At some point
Concentrate
Oh, yeah, that's it

Ramps

Tell me why
I shoulda
Shoulders square
Seem to favor.
Very cold
Take a listen
Many things in me
Break manolo.
Exactly what's need
Is care
& wherever the spit
Settles beg the wind
To breakfast elsewise
Between mean and crest.
Below the depth
Is more surface just as
12'll get you 6 on the
Open market, twice that
This side of
Every step FIRST.
Hill climb
Peek peak
See not.
No C note.
Come to no-no.

Sheep of History

Usually so good
At: getting ahead
Breeze wait up
Just
Miss
Outside
Cross fingers
No one call for
Jam shot
Thar be no grace note in that boots
Filigree damn near
High tails
Since when that's was
Close that door you dope!
Intimacy a backward
Glean in the jailkeep's
Slush bucket
Deuce
Revits
Mice
Spells

Jailkeep's Slush Bucket

They say: twisted
They say: taut
They say: mind the mind
They say: solitary is the truth
They say: such is such
Is some
What makes takes

Finicky shadowy sunlight lite
Keeps on going: lite
No my way: lite

Overcast cloudy
Slight
off plate: lite
Inside
more corner: lite

Riven in sand

In as much as
Et ut quam ut
Clam up, Henry!

a school boy
a soccer chest
a bilious burro

Even and in
Enclosed yen
´˜ç¬øß´∂ ¥˜´

□□

| | | |

□□□□□
□□□□□

Great ride: weather

From inside: out

(Someone

                    laffs)

Some Nice Moola

kind
of
hard
to
do
at
time
gonna
make
catch
underbelly
shower
praise
weather
undirty
yourselves
filters
berry
bones
belts
raise
canals
deport
in
slide
grill
(*duende*)
m*th*r
bleep
h*rps*ch*rd
fills
fjord
wonton
wish
wallows
hadron
collector

wide
open
transparent
mom
and
pop
state
meant
what
meant
drive
it
hoe
field
home
om

Best Whew

all
look
back

Gus!
Bill!
Jean!

Touchibly soft feet
We do't knew
Many a doggie

sucks
left
girdles

'n' alibi stuck
As sign meaning
Meandering

take
a
thankyou
never
4
granted

Love to
Do with this

Tues Looks Wet

Same people
Going thru our heads
Hey, slow children!
Take a break!
Have a Colatata
Born to supplicate
Make mooollllaaa not . . .
Oh, u kno th tally (>>)
If six figures then . . .
I'd'd'd'd'dd'd'd'd'd

Spirits Delivery System

No shame no
B ·°›‹€⁄Ï±’ ·°‡

Sitting in bed
Gonna take my . . .
Goon fever feathers
Adroit ophthamoolinarian

Coupé

Durst de diddly skint
Doost ab idbly twinp

Situation
Have to deal with

Strange device

Go in and read
Your comic books

Clean bills

Giant ant music
Come in, Car B

Direction SW

Growing pains
Joints far free

Senza weather

[Missing Image]

Say it

Copathic incubator on frits
Spastic accelerator fully functionless

Ego, there you go . . .

Tooling along as if in school

roundabout / round up
round of fiddlers playing golf

Ergo suit, $486.98

One salad
Too far

A car dog

Looksee

Craven raven
ugly offa morning, beet dive

Preposition escapade

Loopy cloudy whirr
we later learn

as in

Toodaloo, toodallay
Don't pretend to be

flint, zipper, crust

. . . see you take two tbsp. cumin

and an pinch of . . .

an?

swill down hard
lower rafter, roofbeams!

Sharp
Corner clouds

Frequency beefsteaks

port pro
fessional able

Comfy air
Circle correct answer

Smoke
Nice feeling
Softly

deftly defer
supply rings
hoppity, hippity, plop

Single malted
Shook with

inhering dream
soldier as spun

giblet, giblet who got

Sultan says stop
Slutan says run
Sualntan say ingress
S;ultan s;; whiff

Instant savings
(Call it work)

Airy i.d. ideas

r.r.r.r.r.r.r.r.rr.

heart thisaway

tip

whichawaythatawaykissawayslapaway

Tent here
Get view
Putupwith

[cut the]

Home way from Jerome

It takes a
Wrist watch it

Go up in frames

§§§§§§§§§§§§§§§§§§§§
∞∞∞∞∞∞∞∞∞∞∞∞∞
¶¶¶¶¶¶¶¶¶¶¶¶¶¶¶¶¶¶¶¶
••••••••••••••••••••

off
thumb
come
up
with
game
hang
balance
nothing
bothers
people's
projects

likely
fast
put
back
way
suppose
to
been
one
day
early
skips
bat
likens
indigo
slate
for
months
mill
torrent
flecks
timber
tips
go
sink
barreled
cure
detonate
surrogate
mop
llama's
flame

bring
me
2
ft
comes
down

2
dis

What R U
Fee   Long
Little ling

White shirt
In business
Say HI!

this
isn't
easy
4
easy
2
swallow
table
et
always
B
U

Me
And my big mouth
Alice, and Jerry

Wotan, Millicent, Buckeye
Listen out to steam of
Visiblation, occlumation

gh ghg gh ghgh
jjkkkk oooooo ()
≈≈≈≈≈≈≈≈≈≈
{{``interiority///}}
ablest abreastment
phase maker
by gosh!

(itsy bitsy sudsy couscous)

Alice, Jim, Al, Jack, Frieda

cumquat

(Kuwait?)

give me that old-time permission
give me that old-time permission
it's good enough for me

One of everybody
Care what said
And lastly

Spot Debris

Hasn't [ran] or {drove}

(two second pause)

More doggies
Visible passengers
| | Bring up passengers | |

(proceed to)

Morning gold standard

Scratch moonlight
Head for exit
Tell name

Bitter divide replay

as in:
coax the *!**!! out of the &!!@#$
::: say what you went and did done did

after all: a gherkin is just a small pickle
and not a sleeveless flounce nor
the guy who pushed his nose in
your face one time was more than enough
I can tell you that

Ask your doctor
Well, doc, what it is
Up 2 U

Here there
Here there
Here   there

Wanna go 4 ride
This gets inneresting
Ow's da chicken

Putter whooooo innnnnn
Futtering a roundabout
C meant mix her
Trash basket
Wasting away
Not a what a exactly
Jin mind
Skies dark jin NE

They call me Mr. Gum

up the

Lobster Bisque
(lots of risk)

2 tubes
5 ammonia
3 towel
1 fructify
8 clock
6 dowels

CAUTION: MARINER APPROACHING

Skeet along, as shake is blued
Spelt touch is howdy do
Increase vellum, thwart clue

Scenario screwballs
Run as
electable screws

Fill with
cabinet rejoinders

Peat Moss

I sew
+Eye saw+
Isomorph
(Iceland)
I land
I so and sewn
Eye say
Aye aye
– By ear –
Close by
| Near bye |
Eyesore
I soar
= Eyes spies =
Your eyes
In books
Gulp spire
)Get paid(
All books written
Just ask
[New chapter ready]
World record
How refuse
^We need^
Your help
Put yourself
$$Aside$$
Save up to
50%
Search or
#Shouldna done it#
Funk glower
Bead headwaters
Harsh gurgles
Not roll over
Set slower
This is Cheryl

Hard unnerstan
<Gist is best>
Quik response monitor
Mildewed crest
Say MEOW
~When you can~
Door speak openly
Will call
(Proud)
Force of hand
Tithe the floor

On to something
>>Many others

Never thought about that

#MakeImpact
+GoToJail
=FindFame
*GetOnBus
>Float in balloon
to a mysterious tune

Look Washington

#GabardineLink

Today do clauses
Number looking
Point make
2 PC coffee set

}}Causeway to the stairs{{

Is a cabaret
Like that lifestyle

Don't tell anybody

Nobody listening
Let me tell you

Once I saw the jibberjabber
Dancing on the moon
Dipped so low, jumped so high

Fortune is a squirrel looking for

As we go looping, as we go limping
Fed by our wandering, free of

Something inside
Hard to imagine
Show really good stuff

When this over
Contact number
Clectro muse

Somersault Charges

c
o
n
c
e
r
n
4
f
r
i
e
n
d

cuts both ways
e n t r a n c e
since you've been

s
 a
  y

  i
  t

(s e r p e n t i n e)

Counties Over

s
l
o
g
o
f
r
I
e
n
d
g
l
o

W

Night's sprain ankle
Twist same way
Picture of sunroses

O, no
U suffer shall
Winkle skull

I had a little halo
I made it out of clay

O
r
g
A
n
i
s
m

p
r
e
c
O
n
c
I
o
s
h
oo
d

Irresobbale irredelution

HITS
me in the

cusp

(as slate'll heave it)

e
y
e
s
h
a
v
e
y
e
s
,
v
e
i
t

e
y
e
h
a
v
e
i
t

airborne

Canary in Coal

Swoon into noun
On the way out
But about

Gotta have M um
1 day U re
U R double U

Teflons flummox
Real ox
Lights D do

D dee
Cheese stands X
Rue JJ R innocent

Element (√)
Sobriquet (√)
Lace Sation (√√)

In Z 2 crawl
Back of Q (mation)
Formulary 01742

Eat
On the run
Walking

Sort of Jokingly

Call 922
Fat fingers
Memo: lose lbs

The rest is up to rest
Pazing a says fleur
Help pay what don't

Mean no nothing no way
Got the bonanza
Fleet is swift

By gaze goes thward
Into gym sing era
Fermentation gain

Grab and go
Hands free
Outer sight

Pocketless crescent
Clickety click entry moonlight
Awaken au jus juicy

Policy: cancellation nomination
Jurisdiction: under study
Identity: pretending

Surface marrow
Wake-away plan, no up payment
Flued un cap

Orange paper tablecloth
Musical didi dahdah
End on brush

Lot of do
West with hebrew
Stollen heart gewgaw

Dippity but wait
Weather call in
You're all in

Good day B clean
Early hot air
Pen A/C missive

I got the muscle
Got crepuscular animation
Get joined at sip

Forwentworth shiver mm
Sleeve deboat scrim
Neuter sloth capitulated

Oh, so good
First breath
Bad ass

A place
You wanna wanna
Spend time ime

Fulfilling gradient supply
Sloppy make-up arrondissement
Eleven minutes to infancy

Clock it or (∫0) (¡') (×fi) s'lll
Wages decline in (ø) (•••)
This elicits "—" [ref. 27.4$$3]

Easy cheesy
What's with lights
GH not TE

[*Gesundheit*!
When 'ere she come to
Form where quickens]

Cut lo
Wake U P
Stand alone HUT

Foretaste of power
Apostasy on auction block
Shames protuber rancid

Raus mit die mope
Wherefore the getting smaller
Beepbeep your ass

Classic elegant tasteful
This much giiiving
Really nice lady cry

Fiddleyhowhow
Goldilocks hair & all
Whowhowhowho

It's the grieve up the schlep
Oaken casket is my amulet
Seldom, alligator, breeze

What's that thing in whatshisname
Where guy gives long speech
Sol and Lil pun queasy

People across country
Run X country
Meta mare scarum

Via *de rigueur*, baby!
Schshlllohmo, my pal!
!!!++++???÷÷????>>

Scrotum equals drag
Bounce on skinny dip
Say so said so do so

Doe see dough
Long way hello
Take back step

Oops, excuse
Humid oid
Da babble mess, a nigh

Wanna really dance?
Play dice, dictate oriole
Bubble, trouble, avec boils

The grandeur of my candor
Quixotic as the tumbler
Of mine oncle

Take a test drive
Muscle cardboard
Inside delivery

Lift dat dit
Vasn't dat hat
On da train drain

Recalling: krk*o*pvú
Issue @ jtkîÿ*x*ú
Inassuch as – h*q*q*øœb

Hold on tight!
Veering true downward
In my tiny cupboard

Things R
M prove
Cool waawaa

Back off from
Oh, fuck it
No good noun to

Butter that beyond
Bounce to curveball
At a stretch, right?

Left, your aunt is a big
Flotsam of porridge
So it so it so it so it so it

Orange snatch truck
Cerulean tote avec
Fank U, caw encore

Peps a poison up
Reassemble
Sounds in QT

Bellini scare-monger
À trot de chord
Fromage in, frontage out

RUN DOWN? NO PEP BECAUSE OF TIRED BLOOD? *FEEL STRONGER FASTER!* WITH . . . GERITOL

Mental summer house
Lunch nap
Back to back beach

45 done donuts
Leaf shadow sprinkles
Big question frowntain

Satellite atop phonodisc
Spellers with mint lips
OhOhOHohOhOHoh

Safely in the whisp
Gets beer batter ready
Flimsy fruit bucket ticking

Mustard fall
Back to sleep
Pillow piccolo

Nearing endingly (huh?)
Wing flail
Wheaten statutes

ffffffffffffffffffffffff
jjjjjjjjjjjjjjjjjjjjj
tttttttttttttttttttttttt

No way, Irving!
Get outta the picture
I can’t see the blank!

She’s a niblet
Not a slur
Some hint miss

A winner bump
Bright cloudless morning
Mom’s name

Or did you mean *blink*
vvvvvv
rrrrrrrrrrrrrrrrr

nnnnnnnnnnnnnn
Can you read me, over.
The colonel is in the green room.

This
Cat
Don't
Mooooove

Ear flick
Black mat
Look up

as *like* as like *is* as
for what *in* who
for *or* of at

such cinders send
awake to moth
surly dunk's swathe

Skipping breakfast
Down the street
Stop curb

Bellowing I wants
Gets, neighs, saturates
Flummox times zero

Morning bank shot
Forget keys
Better get a letter

In the cat's bah bah blah
Oakland of the mist
Fum, fud, giggle

Breeze frizz
Stuff puffs
Look numbers

Or an or an Oran
Swear you're sweet
And asway we go

Numbers jump
HQ to U2
5 day Camp Pain

Tripping out on Kant
Lazy Susan spindle
Arrivante detonator

Give us hope
Gled them out
Plead fect

Not feet, you dolt
Seums by
Imp prove corduroy

Array around pitfall
Jimmy, Jimmy, Jimmy!
Argues for arrears

Slick knickers on that jacket
Sez whose is the fate of
Darn near crush in fall

Red
Gets a ticket
Hey, slo down

People always mean well
She need me
A raving thing

CA$H 4 CAR$
ANY YEAR ANY MAKE ANY CONDITION
FREE TOWING

Surreptitiously grasping
Last straws for chocolate
Malted: *Make mine double*

How U been
What'll it B
Here on in

A house made of hands
Grammars pro teams
A land of rara BEAUT

In dar graven imagelesshoodly
Go dust in bitter harze
Flooooon in sppppr

UuUUUuuUuUuUuUU
SsSSsssssSSSuuuuuu
Spray on lawn sputtering

Busy busy day
Happy happy suck
Opera tune

Breathe by all camel
Pretty pretty implant hip
Pay up, pal, by pen

Are in the dole drums
Fêted with pretty cheese
Go in quest of questions!

Entananggled in breeze
Bare the very body
You cannot unlive

Yakative wallpaper
E go less mower
Marvelous littler TC

Magic moment media mothers
They bring in boatloads
Marry El Sound Bite refugees

Gossamer, nah
More than muck for sure
Silent in pupillary

Radiance (folks attest)
Brown-eyes lounge
Lunging any which

Look it the sky
Mind make up maybe
South thru shallow H2O

Selling eyes
They have it
The apropos it

Back in the room
Evening odder rumors
Brain fast break

Fucken decrepit vessel
Chock full a adjectives
Public first time nouns

R me get older
Me active
Loved one love

Spilt in vowels
(1) Carburetor rotate
(2) Inexhaustible

(&) Flux terminal
(^) Oh & by the way
(5) Peaches have pits

Stoke grizzly adamancy
Locked on RV pickling
Moe, Leery, and Curled

From deep space to our place
Polaroid Land Cameras
Over the hills & everywhere

SPIEGEL'S FALL CATALOG
THAT'S SPIEGEL ...
CHICAGO 9, ILLINOIS

Such baggage
We got polls this week
Little big news

Cardio Theater

Big sell-off
double-gangers spin in art of
triage
•fluoroscope
•maximum end-run
•tractor parts
Little bitty ole lady
How U lie cake at
Can talk walk about
IGNORE DOOR
People bespoke
Width IT'S GREAT
glamour and all that
haze of trying
lobs
fulgent efflorescence
git gbl sm lqr grrrr
in
so
far
as
Got to
(Sheesh)
Get mow go
(plasticize bindery)
Not
➔=>>
Home yet
::fell on
This means
(*hold that thought*)
So this means
+got it++
Work
Mentally
Time
ashram

No have
share

à +*guh guh guh*

temp
U
Vamp
"n"
rococococococococoo

Oh, I think
Looking for
Wings, stuff

Search
For
Clues
No
Intel
Now, what nada

The other guy
Louis
He got it

Bounce off
Temp layers
Short break

Sleepy
Then, talking
Talking turnkey

thump thump thump thump thump
thump thump thump thump thump
thump thump thump thump thump
thump thump thump thump thump thump

Layers temp
Break short
Taking, then
Tacking tourney

Got got got it get it got got get it
Got get it, got, go, got, get it
Get it, go, got, got it, it got
It ti ti it titit tit titit itititi

®©
Σ%off
BÛŸ ŃÒW
http://u.to.KY.gel

PICTURE SUNRISE
TOO MANY MOVIES
LIKE A JOB

Rime and Raison

No health questions
Way to go
R X T X D

Stairway

"Let's settle this outside"

Filled with rip tide
Stasis is stun
Hereby question even

One a round

Tha pahk
she's got gas
Well, step on it

Pop loves dementia
Smartest guy on TV
To knowing beyondish

No stealth bullions
Haze of the went
Bubblebubbletoilandtrouble

(Papa love mambo)
(Couple of bridges too far)

"Not in a million years," Fred said.
And now take a look see.

New mump city fie
Leaf wending along longueur
Mark private didiot
Bleak runt of Fall

As our reader digests
(Band of gold)
A lotta white men
Ask WHY?
cat and mouse
Well travel is it warm

Rime & Reason @TheCourse 1 hour ago
Join the campaign for #CageFreePoetry

I'll tell u y: that's y
Don't tell me that
I told you so: so what?

Feigned hunt for trace of fire
Filament of pedigree
Solo for now [void]

Slowing down plan
Alien settlements
Don't . . . , hey waiter!

Meatloaf wafts
Spring twilight
Sidling up to great

Nothing to say
To nobody
Make niiiiiiiiiiice

singly or in plectrums
strum of day
meddlesome ants

beyond fray of . . .

Jeeze, Louise!

there really is a . . .

wanna willa whatta getta

chorus: ___________

____

____

nice suchwise
nice fit

Music says music
Next-to-last blue

than what

Too much wattage

Gotcha mem
and then and then
Ikons

Comes upon us
On this morn
Panfry moonbeams

Celebinebriation pronto
Flowent fiduciary
Flaming gogogogo

I thought I could I thought I could
I thought I could I thought I could
I thought I could I thought I could
I thought I could I thought I could
I thought I could I thought I could
I thought I could I thought I could

I thought I could I thought I could
I thought I could I thought I could

nailed it
(nails it)

lay a glove on her and

LAY AWAY PLAN NO $$$ DOWN DELIVERY TOMORROW IF YOU ORDER IN 23 MIN.

Condopushcart
Big money queens
Attack wakes

Wellspoken Strange

Nearby sundown
Folded foliage
And here's why
e
y
e
b
a
l
l
s

r
o
l
l

Cash register

Dative presence

Fumbling for the keys that day it was almost as if Jessie had been expecting me to take the bait but I knew something was wrong I could smell it that slightly burnt taste like molasses cooked too long in a fry pan or the

what R U hearing when just lean against the wind too strong it can almost knock U over with a forces remind the alphabet the campaign believes it in raw total votes slightly nuts to try and win out there and removes the table with the strong natural finish Ina state this big and says party unity speaks a nice suit in the oppo world with crazy boss pulling hair out these are the all sort a things a great concern unmitigate unfavorables because the press releases never deliver from the Big Town

lightly burned
someone wronged
it's just about

unsightly cashews
unsalted and wound
spoken nicked suite

need
need
need

Take in movie
For an orphan
Dawn went weewee

Kwinakayak pole

tugging at my hurt strings

♫ Oh do you know the roofing man the roofing man the roofing man oh do you know the roofing man who lives on Koalaoula Bay? Yes I've met the toothless lamb the ruthless scum the sifted scam, yes I've met the goofing jam who lives on Symptomaticism Bay. ♫

>>>><<<<<

Deeply sadden
Knew the champ
Knew the champ
Knew the champ

Deeply sadden
Makes us rev
Makes us rev
Makes us rev

Oh

This is

Beautiful

That's the kind
Of guy was
Ali
—June 4, 2016
>>>><<<<<

Apodictics

Fire is hot. First
comes after. Judg-
ment is a kind
of saying. Loos-
en the snare. Pre-
tend you're in
the middle
of. Argument is
part context, part
intent. Stay close,
think far. You've
done it. Sufff-
fer now. Dump
on main drag. Back
in olden gol-
den. You're getting
warmer. Eye out
for bad guys. And
belle galls. How
R U, dwarfling. Needle
help? Present breeze
exception. Start
righting. The
ship. The
old times. Turn
2. Ter-
rible. Well past
1/2. Gradient
mystified. Sell off
right now. Born
over and o-
ver again. Needle
haystack with
ploys. Vent is
now installed.
Wait it off. Seer-
sucker is the bbb-

est sucker. IN
WHICH. Get
it. Some call
it. Land
line. Weather
questions. The docs
are in. Say what,
Doc. Dogs
sniff poems. Folks
heading out. Where's
the fire. That's
what this is about. That's
what we do. It's
all about cars. Out
of New York. Liv-
ing legend. Crowd
source. Goodlier
jolt. Feathered jittt-
ters make for. Out
three and a quarter.
Filleted filter. Air is
combustible. 5 ≠
2. Unless. Numbb-
ers are funny. Audit
thyself. Lettters
crumble / spaces
between are
torqued. Vision is
sight without
cargo. Prognostic-
ation is the art of
procrastination. A day
hey don't go by. It is
what it is. No charges
file. We're getting
there. All epi-
soda. Keys
throw. Twins
twice remove. What

it takes. So many
things. In
motion. Cable news
fantasy. The bird
in handy. Face off
supporters. Sea-
scape deep back-
ground. Under bridge
Z. Family roots
familiar. Enhance
risk area. Rooks familiar
air. Heats linear be
gin. Guts in tow.
That ((p->r)
->((q->r is not
this)->)). THE
PREMISE "SWAT"
IS NOT WELL
-FORMED. Dabbb-
fling in locomotion.
What you know may
not be true and what
is trucked may not
arrive. THE
PREMISE "MAR-
GIN" IS NOT WELL
-FORMED. Absolve
is not reason enough
for freedom. Under-
standing is a dig. Fin
digits. With the judge
width. To blue col
lar white americans. Have
for profit. Merits of the
case. Did appoint
same judge. If
you tell me. I
really don't think. Run-
ning his mouth. Grrr-

ieves me nought. Sugar
in as much as livers
don't fly. "I do declare,
Millicent, that the taste
of the toddy is far from
what it once were." —
We all are. Truth is
foreign. "Damn the facts,
I saw what I saw."
The straightest line
curves at absolute
ballast.

Unnerstan Exakly

everyone's
young
as
they're
young
as
they
are
blind
light
slashes
do
dance
don't
preposition
puppy
luck
daily
slower
walk
take
a
place
wind
up
tight
rope-a-dope
ghost
dive
dance
(premise)
it'll
sloop
that
thistle
in
dry-dock

flittering
along
silicon
doilies
for
grade
sticker
in
quell's
command
fixation
sink
a
drop
by
crosshairs
flung
to
pleat
saw
lot
of
cool
fans
1/2
spine
oh
pine
scale
up
and
smile
down
scale
pup
you're
a
swell
bunch

best
leave
now
copper
hearted
what
do
U
got
2
spill
baby
body
of
truth
hot
day
sweet
goat
feed
itchy
hay
chicken
wire
we
R
well
overdue
nature
copies
itself
stand
in
corner
dunce
butter
shape
N
shimmy

that
wicker
laden
crest
bets
lot
on
lark
sins
of
elevation
slams
tap
tensile
wag
flux
on
blemish
splash
crane
omnibus
lookout
minions
by
bellicose
amend
trait
permeates
awkward
shift
pelts
mills
suck

Back It Up

Say hi to Dustin Allergies
The he who
Guy behind the him, no kidding

There's this way
Some dare call it unselling
No one else waiting

Folds the pranks
Get to the he hoe
Say hit the letch

Begets my pap
That Phillips head
Spews lather on

Ponds of prehensive
Pretense, perimotor
Romp, cohabitation

Invective I'd've left
At Lost Luggage
1932. The wings have

Sparrows, quit the
Horn-rims and
Come as you'd

Like to be and
After a while
Will have been

Tent here
Get view
Put up with

Family vacation
Our people diff
Finger talking point

Past
The thinking about it part
Just a car

What'd she say
Oh, shit
Moon out, yet

Beautiful LAAAADY
Could could Jerry
See ya in a little bit

¿Unsettling? Skip to my
Queue, the better to
Darn those damn

Unicorn holes in the
Belfry: Jack O Lanterns
Swaying in mythic

Miasma, my – no! –
Ashma. Treason?
Trees on what?

Focus before you
Forget, fiddle with
Griddle, yessiree

Pee on porches
That other guy
Few less verandah

Glad
You said that what
Holy Cow!

A capsule here and now
The way back when
MN-CA kill list

Air feels so nice
Even in tweet world
Bkgrd foggy bridge

Breaks across erroneous
Highway, juggling circumstance
Like there was no yesterday

Felt and rubber buffer
Holier excavations, as in
Bride adores a bridge

Fumbles basic ineptitude
As in opportunity knocks
But sometimes only the

Dog can hear it, even
Then, even Steven
Even you, who

Plate lot
100% mere cash
Moonpie inventory

Foot thing
The/a room on 3
Call now

Too much nuancsicle
And you're saying
Wanted 2 vote 4

Sit down, Oh ye Allover
Read code
Hum a reminder Oh No!

Not semiconductor! I paid
At the office. Yeah, yeh
Yup. More silent than

A bowl of balloons. Shrunk
Skull, mirrored foretaste
Gummed-up hairdo

Location uncertain
Dead center of middle
Of edge of periphery

I, & not an angel.
I, & not a seraph.
I, & not a messenger

Morphine floor too polish
Bad mouth world
Hey (sans it) check out

Barometer and then *boing*
Decimating bellwether
Fearless accessory

R whooooooo
Thumb thumb
6 episodas FRAUGHT

Gray grey gray grey
Gray gray grey gray
Gray gray grey gray

Pretty warm
Less on tha pretty
More cheops

More later: took out
Garbage and parked
Truck good till

Threshold NJ
Garners, you think?
Likely to hit

U owe MEOW
(Frown when)
Maybe. Chance of

Sultry episodes, oh . . .
Showers, lid on crooked
Fate as when the

Bate and tackle
Arms flailing
Paintbrush into lox

Who anymore
Forgets his *&^%$
Even has Bro Pockets

Elegant in its own
Lotto pans
Off the handle

These days
(Subtle, now)
Don't no have YO!

Slightest intent to
Gooder thoughts
Instanter, buddy!

Make water wetter
In the rainbow spout
One con tin sinuous strand

Flushed in pensiveness
Watching the images
Dry like ice

Any advice?
Code out for bid
Message cloud and clear

Debating in or about
Snow cap mountain
Goes POP!

Where the words from
I guessed
Forget the {?}

Wampum, Buddy
Bleak snow
Tears impossible

Bare visible
Darling
Down the block idling

Until the Real Thing Comes Around

I'd settle for half that.
Nowhere not spoken for.
Epistemology is to monkeys

What ontology is to parakeets.

Dress Down
 4
Neighborhoodie

Ring arose
Hedge topiary feet
As a stick figurative

Do the old adage
Foxy coming with
Numnum

Doing all right
Okay, green
Turn, uh

Okay left (all cap)

Danger where *de rigueur*
Frowns on proscenium forage
Alligator in, foxglove serendipity

To make or
Say when metal
Says when

♫ Walking my baby down the street
When the band's playing O so sweet ♫

In the middle of the fight
Frantically punching . . .

Not only never saw it
Never dreamed it, never spoke it
Never thought it

(July 2, 2015 – June 11, 2016)

ROOF BOOKS

the best in language since 1976

Books by Ted Greenwald and Charles Bernstein:

Ted Greenwald

A Mammal of Style

in collaboration with Kit Robinson (2013)

Jumping the Line (1999)

Charles Bernstein

Politics of Poetic Form (ed., 1989)

Islets / Irritations

(1992, originally published by Jordan Davies 1983)

Occurrence of Tune

in collaboration with Susan Bee (1981)

Legend

in collaboration with Ron Silliman,

Steve McCaffery, Ray DiPalma & Bruce Andrews

(1980 published with L=A=N=G=U=A=G=E)

Controlling Interests (1979)

Roof Books are published by Segue Foundation

300 Bowery • New York, NY 10012

For a complete list, please visit roofbooks.com

Roof Books are distributed by

SMALL PRESS DISTRIBUTION

1341 Seventh Street • Berkeley, CA. 94710-1403.

spdbooks.org